D1545091

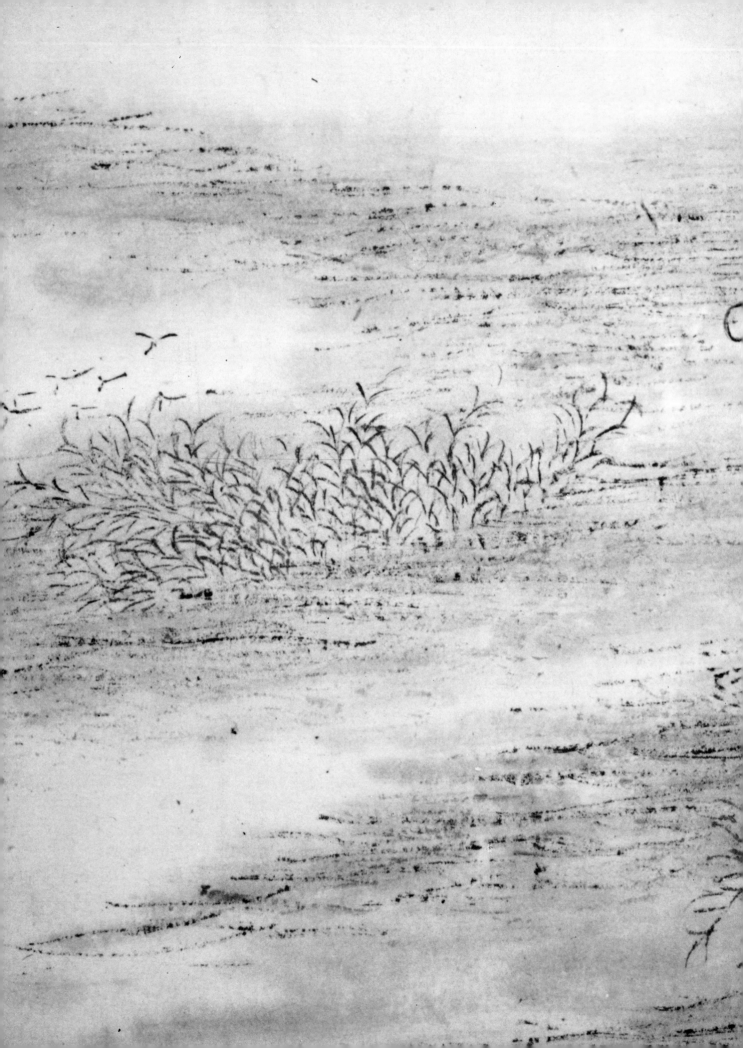

Wandering in Eden

Three Ways to the East Within Us

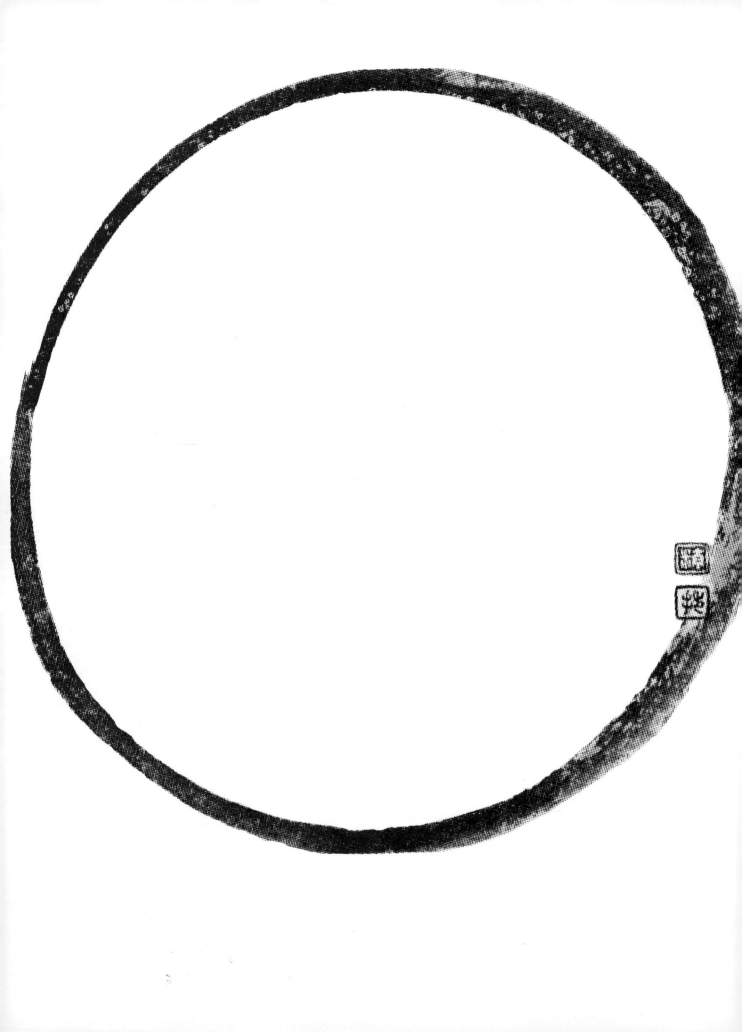

MICHAEL ADAM

Wandering in Eden

Three Ways to the East Within Us

ALFRED A. KNOPF
NEW YORK 1976

THE TITLE *Wandering in Eden* was first that of an extraordinary play by John Fletcher, broadcast by The British Broadcasting Corporation in 1972. The author's agreement to its use here is gratefully acknowledged.

THE FRONT COVER shows a drawing by Paul Reps from one of a series of images with words entitled *Zen Telegrams*. See pages 108, 109.

THE BACK COVER shows a detail from the *Study of a girl with lotus leaves*. Udaipur, ca. 1800. Victoria and Albert Museum, London.

THE TITLE PAGES show numbers 8 and 9 of the traditional *Ten Cow-Herding Pictures*, a series that illustrates the stages by which a man ceases to be ignorant of his true nature. Enlightenment is not to be attained; one's true nature is now and always present (the Kingdom of Heaven is within), but ignorance of it can seem to lessen by stages as a mist gradually clears to reveal what *is*.

Earlier pictures in the series show a man searching for the wild stray cow that represents his true nature (*"She has never gone astray, so what is the use of searching for her?"*); he sees her, catches her, tames her, comes home on her back: *"The struggle is over . . . he sings simple songs of the village boy. Saddling himself on the cow's back, his eyes are fixed on things not of the earth, earthy."* But *"things are one and the cow is symbolic."* The eighth picture shows no man, no cow, only an Empty circle, the image of wholeness; *"All confusion is set aside and serenity alone prevails; even the idea of holiness does not obtain."* But even Emptiness is not an end. *"To return to the Origin, to be back at the Source—already a false step this!"* Nor is Emptiness some Permanent Absolute opposed to the many transient things of the world. *"When he does not identify himself with magic-like transformations, what has he to do with artificialities of self-discipline? The water flows blue, the mountain towers green. Sitting alone, he observes things undergoing changes"* (picture 9). Sitting alone is not an end. Observing is not an end. The tenth and last picture (see page 104) shows the man entering the city, where he will be found in the company of wine-bibbers and butchers.

The complete series of pictures with accompanying verses, and a full explanation and commentary, will be found in *Essays in Zen Buddhism* (First Series) by D. T. Suzuki.

THIS IS A BORZOI BOOK
PUBLISHED BY ALFRED A. KNOPF, INC.

Library of Congress Cataloging in Publication Data

Adam, Michael.
Wandering in Eden.

1. Philosophy, Oriental.   2. East and West.
3. Zen Buddhism.   4. Art, Oriental.   5. Religions.
I. Title.
B121.A3 1976   181   75-34287
ISBN 0-394-49980-8

Manufactured in the United States of America

FIRST EDITION

To EYA, NOAH, SHANE,
to NANCY WILSON ROSS,
& to TOINETTE REES
with gratitude for her part

CONTENTS

Wandering in Eden
Three Ways to the East Within Us

It seems quite true that the East is at bottom of the spiritual changes we are passing through today. Only this East is not a Tibetan monastery full of mahatmas but, in a sense, lies within us.

C. G. JUNG

[We have to] discover in that East something ancestral in ourselves, something we must bring into the light before we can appease a religious instinct that for the first time in our civilization demands the satisfaction of the whole man.

W. B. YEATS

Within ourselves we have our Eastern aspect, deeply buried and yet still acting as our hidden source of light.

GRAHAM HOWE

1

Introduction

We shall study every philosophy, search through all the scriptures, consult every teacher and practise all spiritual exercises until our minds are swollen with the whole wisdom of the world. But in the end we shall return to the surprising fact that we walk, eat, sleep, feel and breathe, that whether we are deep in thought or idly passing the time of day, we are alive. And when we can know just that to be the supreme experience of religion we shall know the final secret and join in the laughter of the gods. For the gods are laughing at themselves.

ALAN WATTS

WITHIN US—TO THE EAST OF OUR-selves—lies a realm that has been little known to Western man except in dreams that are sometimes radiant, sometimes dread, and always haunting.

This alien, beguiling country is increasingly explored in our time, and not by scholars only but as a matter of life by those who see deadliness as the origin of all other "sins." A need of the East among us can be seen in the glut of Indian gurus, in the coming of roshis from Japan, of lamas from Tibet; it can be heard in strange chants and mantras, smelled in sandalwooded rooms where young men in the pride of life and nubile girls turn to the east on arising, knot their legs, breathe deep and slow in the incensed air, with their bright eyes hooded murmur and repeat *Om mane padme hum.* It is revealed in colored tracts offered in the streets of our cities by shaven-headed youths surprisingly vowed to celibacy in the service of a god whose legend allows him sixteen thousand virgins in a single night. More happily, it shows in brighter dress, bells and flowers, longer hair—ancient symbols of vitality, fresh signs of that love of life which "at any and every level of development is the religious impulse."[1]

That the West should so turn to the East, in whatever wise or foolish ways, must mean that its own tradition has failed to provide a sufficiently whole and contemporaneous vision.

BELOW. Naoko Matsubara : *Hippie.* 20th c.

"What man most passionately wants," said D. H. Lawrence, "is his living wholeness and his living unison, not his own isolate salvation of his 'soul.' Man wants his physical fulfilment first and foremost, since now, once and once only, he is in the flesh and potent. For man, the vast marvel is to be alive. For man, as for flower and beast and bird, the supreme triumph is to be most vividly, most perfectly alive. Whatever the unborn and the dead may know, they cannot know the beauty, the marvel of being alive in the flesh. The dead may look after the afterwards. But the magnificent here and now of life in the flesh is ours, and ours alone, and ours only for a time. We ought to dance with rapture that we should be alive and in the flesh, and part of the living incarnate cosmos."[2]

East as West, the need for wholeness persists, but Western religions, for all their differences, are founded upon a dichotomy, a denial of living wholeness: Man is apart from God above, apart from Nature below, and yet must strive to be godly, to be all that he cannot by nature be.* At the end of his striving man may come to stand in adoration before the throne of God; he can never be one with Him. Such a thought is blasphemy.

Such a thought for Eastern religions is *fact*. For all their differences, Hinduism, Buddhism, Taoism, and Zen all unequivocally declare that the ten thousand things are aspects of One; that the living and dying of these things is the way of Life itself; that the names we give to Reality are at best stammered words for what is inexpressibly All and each of us:

Plants, beasts and men; the mountain forests and
  the mind of Aeschylus
And the mouse in the wall.[3]

Poets and mystics among us have said as much,

---

*The upward-reaching West, with its pointed cathedral spikes and its Faustian striving, has apparently wanted a short-cut to heaven, and in spite of Jesus' statement that the kingdom of heaven is within, this has mostly been envisaged as above the body. . . . Western man, in his ambition to fly out of his body, has identified with the head or, at lowest, with the heart. Orientals, with no less spiritual ambition, have stressed the importance of attaining rootedness in the body first and have cultivated the feeling of the centre of gravity in the belly. CLAUDIO NARANJO : *On the Psychology of Meditation.*

and we have, after all, had Jesus among us. But we dismiss poets as dreamers and save ourselves from Jesus by worship of him. Bowing before a man is a way of avoiding his gaze. Cocks start up to crow whenever a disciple appears. In making a no-man's-land of the earth and lifting the likes of Jesus up and away from us into high heaven, religion has committed us to a life of impossible longing, to the desire and pursuit of a Whole that can never be.

Surprisingly, however, and wonderfully, what Western religions have denied us, our science now offers. By way of material empirical means, science has found that matter is not material only, that there is a Whole whose nature cannot finally be known, for *we are It*. Western science has come in this way to confirm Eastern intuition that man is not a part; he is not apart; he is a Whole in a way that cannot be known, but can be found and may be lived.

Mystery is then at the heart of existence; it is not a supernatural matter, but wholly and only natural, the very Nature of things. The Whole cannot be known and so cannot be named; it is not a thing, it is No-thing. With the aid of modern science we can be less surprised to find that the East gives to Reality such names as *Emptiness, Nothingness, the Void, Space*.

Such words can terrify us. And even if we could accept them as approximate names for the Nameless, they would seem to empty our lives of all meaning. Yet those men of the East who speak most freely of the Void sit most firmly in the world and delight in all appearances. Inspired by Lao Tsu and Chuang Tsu, the world of Chinese art is full of a number of ordinary things lit by the extraordinary attention given to them; its landscapes, serene and full of Emptiness, are similarly lit. Emptiness, it seems, in no way denies the world; on the contrary, delight follows upon Emptiness, as all else does. "If there were no laughter," said Lao Tsu, "the Tao would not be what it is."

There is then some secret here that science has yet to come upon. For all the wonder of their findings, scientists do not sit more firmly or walk more lightly than the rest of us; they do not dance in the space they have cleared of the old beliefs. We have come upon Space, but we have yet to feel at home in it, to celebrate our

4

homecoming. So it is that some scientists have also turned to the East for the full implications of their findings. It is a physicist, Erwin Schroedinger, who has said that "all of us living beings belong together inasmuch as we are all in reality sides or aspects of one single being, which may perhaps in Western terminology be called God, while in the Upanishads its name is Brahman."

The way of Western man started out from the East many centuries ago in answer to an impulse to find a New World, a new Heaven and Earth. We have rested for a while in a world overlooked by a paternalistic God, but still in need of living wholeness we have walked on, and in a world that is round and one, we find ourselves now, naturally and inevitably, heading for the East.

This journey to the East of ourselves is told here in terms of the thought and art of India, China, and Japan. Art is integral to its telling, for this wisdom of the East-in-us is nothing abstract and apart; it has the form of our lives, of the whole body of ourselves, all as surely as the vision of the artist is inseparable from its embodiment in material shape and substance.

In telling of India it is imperative to have this grounding of art for, in contrast to that of China and Japan, the thought of India tends to fly the earth, to turn from the appearances of things. Swami Prabhavananda, head of the Vedanta Society of America, has asserted that "central in Indian philosophy is an overwhelming sense of the evil of physical existence, combined with a search for release from pain and sorrow—and by these two things it is distinguished from the philosophies of any other race or country."[4]

If this is indeed true of Indian philosophy, Indian art—in spite of the many puritan and brahminical apologists—runs counter to it, calling instead for an unflinching look at life in all its aspects, together with a refusal to run. The study of Indian wisdom should be accompanied by a walk in Indian streets; a clear look at both reveals the full reaches of the mind, its splendor and its insufficiency. The study of Indian art suggests a more hale and embracing view.

Plenary views of this kind, most needed now

in the West, are more easily found in Taoist China, and in the form of Zen that had root and flowering there. "The essential of the doctrines known to us as Zen antedate Buddhism. They are implied in Lao Tsu, who was a contemporary of the Buddha in the Far East, and they are implicit in Chuang Tsu."[5] Laughter was at the heart of Zen in late T'ang China; the simplicity, orderliness, and rigors of the life of Zen monks did not preclude occasions of unbuttoned lunacy; indeed, to those living safely this side of the Looking Glass, Zen sages can seem at best inspired idiots. Four centuries later, when the inspiration had gone, Zen was taken to a Japan that was then under samurai rule, to be revived and reshaped there by an unsmiling military spirit.

It is this Japanese form of Zen that asserts itself in the West today and is taken very seriously by some who baldly sit in serried ranks before a roshi with a staff and an image of the Buddha to back him up. Seemingly freed from the forms of Western religion, we can be enslaved by Eastern forms. To take Zen seriously is to miss the point of it. Zen points to *things*—a fly on a windowpane, a dirt scraper, a frog—and so asks that we go wide-eyed about the world, to make of common place a Paradise.

Zen is a Japanese word; it is what the character of that land has made of *Ch'an,* * which is what the Chinese temperament made of the Indian *Dhyana,* when wedded to its native Taoism. What the West will make of its inheritance of Zen remains to be seen. The adoption of old beliefs, the aping of alien ways, is invariably comic when it is not so clearly tragic. If there is worth in Zen, it is because it is of worth beyond all words, even in spite of them, as of all forms Eastern as Western. We may journey to the East but at peril of our liveliness we must not halt there. Our want is not to become Eastern but to be whole, "alive to all that is enjoyed and all that is endured." The way of avoidance and withdrawal associated with much Eastern

* "Becoming one with the universe" is the literal connotation of the character *ch'an* of Zen (i.e., Ch'an): it is composed of *tan* (one, singleness) and *shih* (sun, moon, and stars hanging from Heaven, hence the universe). MAI-MAI SZE : *The Tao of Painting.*

thought it not our way, if it is any man's. How shall one withdraw from the world that one is? The Western readiness to translate ideas into acts, to make the Word flesh, is now a need in the East as urgent as any need we may feel for a profounder understanding of the Word itself. The failure of the East is as apparent as that of the West. Both are the consequences of separation and exclusion. East and West are two apparent halves of a whole, as they are two apparent aspects of individual men and women. The need is marriage, within as without. The need for us in the West is, moreover, as Joseph Campbell has written, "not simply to assume uncritically the patterns of the past, but to recognize our own creative possibilities; not to remain on some proven level of earlier biology and sociology, but to represent a movement of the species forward. And this, I would say, is in a particular way the special charge of all who are living today as modern Occidentals, for it is this modern Occidental civilisation which, since the middle of the thirteenth century, has been—quite literally—the only innovating civilisation in the world."[6]

Wisdom does not lie in the East; it lies in each of us, as surely as stupidity does.

This must seem to make the journey to the East unnecessary. So it is. But for many of us it seems necessary to wander in order to find where we are.

We have wandered so far we are haunted now by a sense of exile. The myth of our beginning tells how we grew in a Garden that God once planted "eastward in Eden," but when the time for innocence was past, God played the game that Genesis describes: Assuming the guise of Jehovah, He was as a fond parent pretending to be stern, depriving us of the ease of Eden so that we might grow by gathered strength and gentleness into man- and womanhood. God knew well that to prohibit the Tree of the Knowledge of Good and Evil was the way to make man covet its fruit. Adam could have "put forth his hand and taken also of the Tree of Life," but it would have been premature; mankind can bear Reality only insofar as he is himself real, and know Life only by living it. So, divided in themselves and separated by knowledge of one another as of good and evil

and all other opposites,* Adam and Eve were sent from the enclosure of Eden into the alarming spaces of the world.

Endlessly wandering in search of a way back to the Garden, we may come to the East only to be told that there is no way, and no need of one, for there waits in us always the realization that Eden is not another place but a state of living unison, of being who we are and where, with widest eyes. Paradise is regained in the recognition that it was never lost. We waken from the long dream of having left it and find ourselves at home all the while.

*Like empty space, it has no boundaries
Yet it is right here, ever profound and clear.*[7]

What the East has to tell us is all that *can* be told: We are sleepwalking in Eden and may awaken to it. This can come as a surprise until we recall that the same has been said among us. What else is the meaning of the kingdom of heaven being within us? And of Jesus saying, according to Thomas, that the kingdom of the Father is spread upon the earth, and men do not see it? What else could William Blake have meant by his assertion "If the doors of perception were cleansed, every thing will appear to man as it is, infinite"? Dostoevski said similarly: "Life is Paradise; we are all in Paradise, but we won't see it . . . we don't understand that life is Paradise, for we have only to understand it and all will be fulfilled in all its beauty."[8] And so it was that Dietrich Bonhoeffer in prison before his murder wrote to a friend and urged us all: "Make the most of the beautiful country you are in. Spread *hilaritas* around you, and mind you keep it yourself!"[9]

Eden is in us and about us and in all ways, East as West, we are wandering in Eden.

---

*For Nicholas of Cusa the coincidence of the contradictories, the reconciliation of the opposites is the wall that encloses Paradise, the place where God is found by revelation. *Visio Dei*

OPPOSITE. Felix Hoffmann : *Eden*. 20th c.

REFERENCES

1. LEUBA quoted in *The Varieties of Religious Experience* by WILLIAM JAMES
2. D. H. LAWRENCE : *Apocalypse*
3. ROBINSON JEFFERS : *The Beginning and the End*
4. SWAMI PRABHAVANANDA : *The Spiritual Heritage of India*
5. ALAN WATTS
6. JOSEPH CAMPBELL : *Myths to Live By*
7. YUNGCHIA TASHIH : *Chengtaoke*
8. DOSTOEVSKI : *The Brothers Karamazov*
9. DIETRICH BONHOEFFER : *Letters and Papers from Prison*

The Way of the Body

ABOVE. *Ghandarva* (Celestial musician). 11th c.

1 The Way of the Body

As a man is in his body, so will he be in the world. . . . As a man is in the world, so will he be in the mystery that founds, sustains and engulfs the known world.

SAM KEEN

INDIA HAS FOR LONG HAUNTED THE Western mind as a dream whose meaning seems none the less for being incomprehensible. India is as night to the day of our minds; it is a land of dreams, literally; and well knowing now that dreams can tell intimately of the dreamer, we may be haunted by that other half of ourselves we have kept hidden or have hidden from. India has become a name for all that is other-worldly, even a synonym for the soul.

It is not the soul of India we should seek, but its body we should find, for the body of old India was not a thing apart, nor even a thing of parts: there was no soul or spirit or mind or flesh. There was one Body, and it did not stop at the skin of a man, but comprised the whole Universe, with the sky as head, the sun as eye, air as breath, space as the body, earth as feet.

Wholeness of this kind is now our need. The Christian centuries have by the separation and elevation of the spirit brought insult and bewilderment to the body. Now the body revenges itself at the expense of the spirit, and being separate still is bewildered still. "Eros, who was a god for the Ancients, is a problem for the Moderns," says Denis de Rougement. "The God was winged, charming and secondary; the problem is serious, complex and cumbersome. But this applies only in the West. . . . Why has eroticism become an age-old synonym for perversity not only in the legal jargon of the secular state, but in the eyes of sincere and high-principled Christians?" And how is it that "religious morality and eroticism have reached this state of permanent conflict, of reciprocal contempt, of rigorous mutual exclusion? No such situation prevails in India."

He assumes too much for modern India, since by that he cannot mean its villages alone. In Indian villages men are still to be found standing upright and at ease in all winds; women float red flowers in the rivers of their hair, sway under pitchers of water, bright sunlight on their breasts. But the modern Indian under the influence of the West is only urban and ashamed, goes head first, headlong about his life, his body limping after.

OPPOSITE. *Yakshi* (Dryad). East gate, Sanchi, 1st c.

11

ABOVE. *Meeting of Radha and Krishna* (detail). Kangra, 19th c.

Perhaps it was always so in much of India.* Its art, however, can suggest otherwise. Great temples, sculptures, and small paintings survive to suggest an "India" that truly complements us, that is even in us. The discovery of it now might well find us whole, at ease in ourselves and so with all about us.

We cannot know what these works of art meant to those who made them; what matters is what they can mean to us. Indian art can reveal an attitude toward life that is of relevance to us all, East as West, here and now.

Indian art was not made for art's sake, "It is for love's sake," wrote Ananda Coomaras-

---

*The complexity of sexual attitudes is apparent even from the Vedic age . . . we find the first references there to the forced continence and guilt feelings for which Indian religion and literature are well known. RICHARD LANNOY: *The Speaking Tree*.
Incapable of transcending the flesh [the Hindus] showed their ingenuity in etherealising it. N. C. CHAUDHURI: *The Continent of Circe*.

wamy. Love is the one strong thread upon which all the many kinds and multicolored beads of Indian art may be strung, for it is—from the old Indian point of view—the one and the same love that manifests wherever and whenever, in whatever guise.

For that one love fish follow one another in the deep, snakes in the desert tie themselves in knots, hawks in the high air circle and shriek. For love the stallion mounts the mare. For love a raging sailor seeks the harbor of a whore all the while an adolescent poet searches in a midnight attic for words that will exempt from death his blue-jeaned Juliet, his Cleopatra whose burnished throne is the back seat of an old car. For that same love a man once stood with his arms wide and his hands opened to make a place for nails. And another man by that same love was persuaded to forgo the balm and cloister of a palace, an ardent queen, and the shine of a son, to wander all the land of India once, a begging bowl in his hand.

There are differences in love, but no distinc-

tions. There will seem to be a difference between the winding lust of serpents and the still compassion of a Buddha, but it is the same impelling force that manifests as both serpent and savior. There can even seem to be a sequence that leads from one to the other, a way of love, natural and inevitable as the way of a growing tree, from root to trunk and branch and leaf and flower and fruit. Love is not the fruit alone; it is not an ideal end; it is at the beginning.

"In the beginning," say the Upanishads, "verily all this did not exist. From Non-Being, Being was produced. That Being changed into a Self. Verily in the beginning this Self was alone. There was no other winking thing. This Self thought: 'Let me now create the worlds.' The Self desired: 'Would that I were many. Let me procreate myself.' He warmed himself; he created the world and entered it. Verily he had no pleasure. One alone has no pleasure. He desired a second. He became as large as a woman and a man in close embrace. Then he

divided himself in two. Thereby arose a husband and a wife."

The story continues with the game still played by men and women everywhere: she runs in order to be chased; she hides in order to be found. It is a game as old as creation itself, says the Indian myth. "I will hide," said the first god-woman. She took the guise of a cow. Whereupon the first god-man became a bull and covered her. So cattle were born. The first god-woman hid again in the guise of a mare. He found her and became a stallion, mounted her, and horses were born. She became a ewe, he a ram. So there are sheep in the world. And so it was that all creatures came about, even to the ants; even to all lesser and the least of things.

In this way it is told that the world is not the manufacture of God, but his manifestation. We, as all other creatures, are not the product of God, apart from him; we are his appearance. God is not only everywhere; he is everything. He is everyone. And he is One.

13

From the seeds of their myths of creation, a people's attitudes unfold. If all is God, there will be differences in form, but no divisions; no God apart from the world, no world apart from man, no man apart from all else that is; no spirit apart from matter, no mind apart from body, no religion apart from sex. Sex was the means by which original Being brought about the world, and it was done in the pursuit of pleasure. That sex should have associations at once godly and pleasurable can seem strange to us; it gave rise to an art that is at once sacred *and* sensual, and so profoundly different from our own.

Myths apart, the earliest formulations of Indian thought saw in the love of man and woman a reflection and a symbol of that state wherein the illusory sense of separateness is lost and wholeness is known. Not in symbol only, but on its own level, the act of sex was seen as the experience of Oneness, of original Being. So the Upanishads say: "In the embrace of his beloved a man forgets the whole world—everything both within and without; in the very same way, he who embraces God knows neither within nor without." And further it was said: "God is eternal Bliss." How better shall the meaning of this be suggested than by that ecstasy common to all creatures, man and woman, beast and bird and insect?

Indian art gives shape to such attitudes. The art of the early and medieval periods shows no distinction between the sacred and the profane as we understand them; no separation between God who is Love, and the human/animal four-lettered love. Western critics have until recently shaken their heads over much of Indian art; white men and women in the dark shadows of Indian temples have blushed and hurried by, have abused them, or have stood only to gape and giggle.

On the east coast of India at Konarak stands a temple to the Sun as symbol for the one principle behind all things, for God. A Victorian critic called this temple "the abomination of India." "Frank pornography," said another, sharing the belief of the Christian who wrote that "an ocean of carnality within us continually lashes against the shores of our spiritual natures; and these mighty waves of Carnality and Sensuality drown the voices of the divine within us. The deliverance of the soul from the error of the senses—the lust of the flesh—is salvation."

To stand before Konarak or the temples of Khajuraho with such a mind is to be horrified. These are temples avowedly raised to the glory of God and their walls are carved with blatantly erotic figures, men and women in all imaginable ways of coupling, and some unimaginable ones. That a house of God should so unashamedly celebrate the lust of the flesh, the delight of the eyes, and the pride of life is shocking to Western moralists. These stone libertines are not shown here as the gargoyles and grimacing monsters of our cathedrals; they are not outsiders or only decorative additions; they are the very walls of the temples. The wish to celebrate shaped these figures; they acclaim the part of the body in the play of things. There is no shame here. It may be the lack of shame that shames us.

So many Western critics have halted at the lower half of these figures, have concentrated on genitalia; they have not been able to see the whole figures, certainly they have not seen the faces—blissful, smiling, calm. The figures are sexually active, but they are not obsessed; they are at ease; they are in the world but not of it; they play.

This appearance of lively activity about a hub of calm is characteristic of Indian images; the "still point" is shown together with the "turning world." It is also the character of Indian architecture. The erotic carvings crowd the outer walls. As one walks into the temple itself, the images are found to be sensual still and full of grace, as befits the dancers and celestial musicians they represent, but the more obvious eroticism is absent. The figures stand alone. As one moves deeper into the heart of the temple, the figures grow fewer. In some temples they vanish, to be replaced by a tracery of vines and of flower motifs, sometimes abstracted wholly. Increasingly in this way, the pilgrim was led to leave the world of living forms behind and to approach the spirit of those forms, the mystery of love and life itself. He enters a further chamber where all the noise of the world is shut off; very little light penetrates. Here, gone beyond all gods and other men, he pauses to ready himself for the final step. Then, still and as nothing; that is to say, when he is himself in the image of God, he strides into the center of the temple and the heart of himself. It is dark. The four walls are bare. The cell shows nothing. *Nothing.* All imagery and representation is not only impossible now, but even misleading; it is Maya. Here is Nothingness. Here is what the Hindus call Immensity; what the Buddhists call the Void, what the Christian mystic Eckhart intended when he spoke of God as *The Absolute Nothing,* and was excommunicated for it.

From the blatant images of sexual union on the temple sides to the silent inner core there is a progression of sorts: from sensuous form to the ultimate abstraction which the image-making mind can only call Nothingness; beyond all concepts to the experience of a Reality that cannot be conceived, cannot be formulated, shaped, or spoken. But "progress" in the West implies improvement, a movement to something nobler; a scale of values is implied. Progress in the East is a matter of growth, from crude representation to abstraction, from gross to subtle forms of manifestation. But it is the same principle that is manifest. The walls of these temples were carved with the sculptor's care and delight in forms, but the temples as a whole were conceived, planned, and constructed under the direction of priests who, celibate and austere themselves, saw it only fit that a building to celebrate the Creative Principle should include all aspects of creation. Everything has its part to play, its time and its place. So in the sunlight that bathes the outer walls there is sex unashamed; at the center there is silence, darkness, stillness, Nothingness.

The way of Indian art is not one of blind sensuality, as its detractors insist, nor only of "spirituality," as its defenders say. It is a whole way; neither obsession with the world, nor withdrawal from it. It is being in the world, lightly, with a little smile. In that smile lies the secret of this art, as of love and of life itself. Understandably we are haunted by that smile wherever we meet it, in archaic images of Egypt and Chaldea, of China and Japan, in the angels of Rheims—Angels, it is said, are able to fly because they take themselves lightly.[1]

OPPOSITE. *Apsaras* (Heavenly courtesan) *undoing her skirt.*   ABOVE. *Head of Buddha.* Siam, 7th c.
Bhuvaneshwar, 10th c.

But to come to take things lightly we must first *take* them. We are angels not by avoidance, but by embracing—a man, a woman, a world—with a little smile. It matters foremostly that each one should fulfill himself at his own level. Sexual curiosity was seen in India as one of the main causes of perversity of mind. It was felt that a man should grow to maturity by way of experiences that left no dark corners in him, no "unlived lines." So if and when a man or a woman moves toward the center of his being, as the pilgrim moves toward the center of the temple, he will come to leave behind the limited expression of love that is sex, and do so naturally and inevitably, without secret longings, without looking over his shoulder, since he has lived in and out of the sphere of sexual experience, has fully experienced it, and so is free of it. Sex now ceases to be channeled and identified with particular parts of his body; instead it spreads, informs, irradiates the whole of him. The sage in this way fulfills sex, as the flower fulfills the root.

Himself exempt from the fever of sex, the sage does not condemn those who remain sensually concerned. How could he condemn them when the Creator himself is described in sexual terms? In the beginning was Nothing. Nothing becomes One. One becomes two and these are male and female. It is similarly told in Genesis: "God created man in his own image, in the image of God created he him; male and female created he them." The dissemination of the Bible story has for the most part been the work of male moralists made stern by their fear of women, so that this image of God as male and female has been glossed over.

In India unashamedly, God becomes male and female, and all creation is seen in terms of this polarity: "Of gods, animals and men, the God is all that is called male; the Goddess is all that is termed female. There is nothing else than they."

The whole cosmic process is in this way reflected in the relationship of the sexes, and man and woman in their relationship reflect the cosmic process. Man is the gleam of day as woman is the dark of night. He is a hill, a tree, a

lightning flash; she is a cave, a lake, a cloud of rain. He is sun to the earth of her; the thorn in her thankful flesh. He leaps in the dance, she sways. They are opposites and as such they meet and fuse, and for that while can seem as one; their opposition is resolved in an intimacy where "each is both." As it was in the beginning, so from this One all the many will follow—sons and daughters or creative deeds; the acts and utterances of every day. The outcome is true insofar as the opposition is true. Their togetherness creates lively patterns so long as they maintain their own ways. They are warp and weft; they lie under and over, criss and cross, and the pattern of their lives owes to their different directions. The femininity of Indian women, their otherness to men, is apparent. Women in the West are surely right now to claim equality and freedom in a world that men have dominated, but they are wrong surely to interpret that freedom as the ability to do as men do. It is not that women cannot do as men do; the wonder is that they should want to.

As the cosmic process is mirrored in the relationship of the sexes, so this relationship itself serves as a symbol for the eventual return of the two to the One; union of the individual with God. The several stages of this return can be found in Indian art. The carnality of Konarak can be seen as an early stage: a woman on that temple side bends before her man, who is as an animal upon her—it is the level upon which the simple man experiences Oneness.

A later stage may be seen in the miniature paintings of Northern India, which for the most part tell of incidents in the life of God in his incarnation as Krishna. "God is love," we say, and while this can seem a limited view to the Indian, he would gladly accept it as such, explaining it further by pointing out that the incarnate God, Krishna, made love in a single night to sixteen thousand village girls in the green valley of Vrindavana. This makes clear to

LEFT. *Krishna serenading Radha* (detail). Basholi, 18th c.

OPPOSITE LEFT. *Krishna's round dance.* Jaipur, 18th c.

20

the Indian peasant the extraordinary strength and extent of God's love; omnipotent indeed! It is told in terms that the peasant well understands. And the Indian philosopher, himself enamored of abstractions, finds no quarrel with the statement, knowing for what it stands.

In these paintings, Krishna is sometimes represented as a god with miraculous powers; sometimes in situations that can seem all too human. This apparent confusion between the sacred and the profane only makes clear their identity. So Krishna plays his flute in the still moonlit night, disturbing the dreams of the cowgirls of Vrindavana, who wake and hurry from their husbands' beds to gather about him. This can be understood as the call of a Christ to leave all familiar ties to follow him. But it is presented here in human terms: the longing, simply, of impassioned women for the bright of a man.

A small painting shows the many village girls dancing in a circle, at the center of which is Krishna; it shows him dancing at the same time beside each and every girl. So it is told: the love of God is not abstract, but personal and particular. God loves all men, all things, but also, all the while, he loves each one wholly and only.

Other miniatures show Radha, the particular love of Lord Krishna, at her bath preparing herself for a meeting with him. Her attendants hold cloths to hide her nakedness, but Krishna, being God, has easy ways to overcome such mortal means: he becomes many and so looks on Radha from several vantage points, or he makes himself invisible, so as to delight in the sight of Radha naked.

BELOW. *Radha bathing*. Garhwal, 18th c.

Another picture tells the story of Krishna coming one day upon the girls of Vrindavana bathing in the river. Their clothes are heaped upon the bank. He gathers these and climbs into a tree. The girls see him and lower modestly into the water, begging him to return their clothes. Krishna says that they must come and get them. They do so, trying to shield themselves with their small hands. Krishna laughs and insists that they bare themselves wholly before him. This may be enjoyed as a story; it may as well be seen as the need, also expressed in Western religious literature, for the individual to stand before God, stripped of all possessions and worldly concerns. Indian art shows it literally, and the wide differences in attitudes of East and West can be realized only if Krishna is understood as an incarnation of God, as surely as Jesus among orthodox Christians. The thought of Jesus in such a tree in such a situation might cause surprise, even shock to some, yet we should not be wholly unprepared for it. The writings of the Christian mystics are full of

ABOVE LEFT. *Krishna stealing the milkmaids' clothes.* Rajput, 18th c.

LEFT. *Radha and Krishna by a lotus pool.* Guler, 19th c.

phrasing that is not merely sensual, but even sexual. The poems of St. John of the Cross are erotic in expression, and the sculptor Bernini made the moment of orgasm his model for St. Teresa's experience of union with God. Taking his cue from the saint's own words, he used the transfixed body to represent the soul that is pierced by the coming of Christ, "down to the very bottom of the bowels."

The presence of the Song of Songs in the Bible's midst has embarrassed both Jews and Christians. The serving girl sings: "Let him kiss me with the kisses of his mouth," and her shepherd swain answers: "Thy navel is like a round goblet . . . thy belly is a heap of wheat . . . thy two breasts are like two fawns that are twins of a gazelle." Into such simple phrases has been read the relationship of the Church to Christ; while among the Jews, the thighs are seen as the Torah, the belly as the Book of Leviticus. India would accept such mystical interpretations *and* the simple telling of sensuous love between a man and a woman.

The Christian church speaks of nuns as the brides of Christ. The old Indian artist would have assented gladly to the inner meaning of this, but would also have felt free to paint a nun upon the arms of Jesus, going with him over the Galilean hills as his chosen bride. "He that loveth not knoweth not God," said St. John, for "God is love." So if the Krishna paintings as a series express the longing of the individual soul for God, they also speak all the while of the simple need of men and women for one another. The one want does not deny the other, but only proves how God, who is love, penetrates and permeates all levels of existence, from the most gross and sensual to the most ethereal and abstract.

BELOW. *Radha and Krishna*. Basholi, 18th c.

This literal imagery is carried further in Nepal and Tibet, where images are found of the incarnate gods, each one with his own goddess in his lap. The male figure is seen as the abstract Principle and as such he is unmoving. His female consort in joining with him arouses him and stirs him into activity, so that the Principle for which he stands shall take on substance and be manifest in the world. The Word is made flesh. She is his shakti, his energy, as she is also the material world he enters and makes fruitful. So it is shown how man and woman complement one another, each playing his and her true part for the furtherance of things. Man is as day, woman as night. "Without night," said the poet Rumi, "the nature of Man would receive no income, so there would be nothing for the Day to spend."

Erich Fromm in *The Art of Loving* tells of such things and points out that "the polarity of the male and female principle exists in nature; not only as is obvious in animals and plants, but in the polarity of the two fundamental functions, that of receiving and penetrating. . . . It is the polarity of the earth and rain, of the river and the ocean, of night and day, of darkness and light, of matter and eternity." And he continues: "The polarity between male and female principles exists also within each man and each woman. Just as physiologically man and woman each have hormones of the opposite sex, they are bisexual also in the psychological sense. They carry in themselves the principles of receiving and penetrating, of matter and spirit. Man—and woman—finds union within himself only in the union of his female and male polarity. This polarity is the basis for all creativity."

Indian art shows this further stage in the growing of love's tree by a figure whose left side is feminine, swaying and rounded with a full, soft breast, while the right side is male, upright, chested. Another figure will be found at once phallic and breasted. The one androgynous figure in this way symbolizes the inward marriage to which each man and woman must come. Again, this should not seem strange to us. There are such figures in early Western art,

24

and the recently discovered Gospel according to Thomas, a Coptic text of the second century, has the lines: "They said unto Him: 'Shall we then, being children, enter the Kingdom?' Jesus said: 'When you make the inner as the outer, and the outer as the inner; and the above as the below. . . . And when you make the male and the female into a single one, then shall you enter.'"

The same conception is expressed more abstractly in an object that is found all over India: an upright pillar representing the phallus and called *lingam* is set in an oval base representing the female vulva and called *yoni*. The joining of these two in the one form symbolizes the stage of unity, of Wholeness, seen not in the Freudian sense of a return to the womb, but as a moment of conception, of rebirth.

The mind of the Hindu philosopher is capable of the most fantastic abstractions, but they are made concrete by the artist's translation of them into terms of the human body. The Italian psychoanalyst Ferenczi said that "the derisive remark was once made against psychoanalysis

that the unconscious sees a penis in every convex object and a vagina in every concave one. I find that this sentence well characterizes the facts." The Hindu would agree. In remoter parts of India upright stones placed by the State as boundary markers will be found garlanded with flowers, anointed with oils. For the people of the place the boundary stone is also phallic; as such it clearly manifests the Creative Principle, and so is to be accorded due worship as a sign of the God who is everywhere as every thing—a Buddha, a stone, a tiger, a snake, a bee.

This image of the *lingam* and the *yoni* could seem a final symbol of Unity. The point and purpose of Indian art and thought is, however, not merely to state or celebrate the unity of all things, but to realize it, to experience it; the aim is not information, but transformation.

Reality itself, God, Brahman, the Non-Dual Immensity, the Void—call it what we will—is not finally to be given shape in wood or stone, nor is it told in words. *Neti, Neti,* cry the Upanishads—"Not this. Not this." But together with this ultimate negation goes the final assertion: *Tat tuam asi!* "That art thou!" Reality is not to be described but That are thou! You, the living, seemingly separate being, are the visible form of That which is deathless, invisible, and whole. Human existence is said to be the coordination of the absolute and the relative, of That and thou. Enlightenment is the realization of this Unity.

Indian thought does not therefore stop at the confrontation of man and God, the *I* and the *Thou* of Martin Buber. It calls for union, or, rather, for realization of the union that already exists and has always existed.

Indian art shows the man in whom this realization has taken place in the image of the Bud-

dha. Even as the temple side shows all the whirl of life, its sensual play and its pride, together with an unruffled core, so Indian art offers tumultuous images of many-armed gods and goddesses, some with bloody tongues and necklaces of skulls, of lion- and elephant-headed gods, monkey and serpent gods and goddesses, demons and monsters . . . together with the serene image of the sage, gently smiling.

The Buddha image is not primarily meant to represent a historical figure; it is to show what all men can prove to be, that which they already are, but do not know it. At the end of this way of love stands not a work of art at all, but a living man or woman in whom there has been brought about the necessary inward marriage and consequent union with all things.

There is nowhere to go now, nothing to do, no one to become. Love is not the desire and pursuit of the Whole; it is the Whole. The sage does not squat with the stern resolve of the ascetic, nor move as a cautious monk with his mind at the devil's mercy. Wide-eyed, he sits and walks with the ease of willows and unhurrying streams.

When asked who he was, the Buddha replied: "I am Awake."

27

In seeing these images of Indian art as stages, we have walked from the noise and chaos of the outer walls into the center, into the calm, silent heart of the temple; moving from the simple man whose acrobatic sensuality is portrayed like a frieze whose theme is the Dance of Life, to the sage who is at the still point of the same Dance. But the loudly echoing walls and the silent core are parts of the one temple, not to be separated. Without the enclosing walls there would be no silence, no stillness at the center. So the savage and the sage are aspects of the one God, parts that he plays as an actor upon the temporal stage. Viewed from eternity, the temple with its walls and its center, even as man and God, exists together as one whole; it is only from the standpoint of time that we can see any separation and so speak of movement, of stages from one to the other; it *seems* to take time to move deeper into the temple, into ourselves.

From this standpoint one speaks of growth from the natural man to the sage (who is no less natural; it is we who stand between savage and sage that can seem unnatural and act unnaturally). To symbolize this apparent growth, the Indian has his own Tree of Life. This does not grow in Eden, however, but in ourselves; not far away and long ago, but in our present, here and now. The roots of the tree are set at the base of the spinal column; its flowering is in space above the firmament of the skull. At the base of this tree there also lies a serpent, Kundalini, but this is no evil one.* This is the energy of life, immanent and accessible to all, but sleeping until and unless aroused. Growth in awareness consists in awakening this serpent power and allowing it to ascend the tree of the spine, enlivening as it climbs all the centers of the body: heart, mind, and spirit. At the

*It was God himself who, at the end of his great work, coiled himself up in the form of a serpent at the foot of the Tree. FRIEDRICH NIETZSCHE

base of the spinal tree, the serpent manifests as sexual energy. There is no sin in the Indian view; there is no evil as such. There is energy, which may manifest itself in an apparently evil manner when thwarted or repressed. Western psychology, as its history, confirms this.

Kundalini, the serpent power, is Eros. Eros is more than only sexual, but it is also other than an ideal, bodiless love. Eros is love in the whole body that may or may not have sexual expression; it is quite other than what is well called "sex-in-the-head," as far from pornography as from prudery. Eros is the energy of life, and Denis de Rougement has suggested that "The conversion of the energy of Eros will perhaps one day reveal itself as more important for the future of humanity than the present domestication of nuclear power and solar energy. For if the latter is to permit us to explore cosmic space and to provide for the feeding of the body, the former can permit the mind to explore the little-known riches of animistic space and time, and to find in them substance to nourish newly awakened hungers of another kind."

Such a conversion of the energy of Eros is not, from the Indian view, to be seen as an evolution. Heinrich Zimmer has pointed out that the proper metaphor for the Indian view of the process of fulfillment is not that of progress, growth, evolution, or expansion into greater external spheres, but "Self-recollection." The savage or natural man in becoming a sage "brings into consciousness what already lies in a hidden state, dormant and quiescent, as the timeless reality of his being." So we in the West have been told: "Be still and know that I am God."

We have also been told that if we seek, we shall find. The Indian, however, is warned not to believe him who claims to have sought and found, only him who has found without seeking. God is not to be sought, only to be found. Asked for evidence of God, the sage may point to a man, a robin, a rat, a fly on a dung pat. *Tat tuam asi.* This is not, however, to say that any creature is God. *Neti, Neti.* Not this! Not that! But we are no less mistaken if we lift our eyes heavenward or close them and look for God elsewhere than on the earth and its creatures. *Iti! Iti!* "It is here! It is here!"

ABOVE. *The boy Krishna dancing on Kaliya the Serpent.* 16th–17th c. Called to protect the village folk from the menace of Kaliya, Krishna dances on the Serpent's head to show his easy mastery of evil. He does not destroy Kaliya for, as in a good drama, evil has its place and part to play.

OPPOSITE LEFT. Yogini with serpentine energy issuing from her vulva. South India, 19th c. Energy that at root manifests sexually will, if allowed to rise unobstructed, have flowering in the man or woman who is Whole. So Tantric Buddhism states: *Buddhahood resides in the vulva of woman*—the man's view; the corresponding worship of the *lingam* is woman's expression of this.
OPPOSITE RIGHT. Snakes (cosmic energy) coiled about an invisible *lingam.*

The stillness of God is not apart from the dance of our every day; it is at the heart of it. In T. S. Eliot's words, "except for the still point there would be no dance" and "there is only the Dance." It is not by leaving the world that we come upon the heart of it, nor by refusing to dance that we come upon stillness. On the contrary, it is by abandoning ourselves to the dance, by living fully and fearlessly at each and every stage of ourselves that we move naturally and inevitably to the next stage; or rather, we find ourselves moved, as the bud finds itself a flower, or the ungainly caterpillar is suddenly and without intent a winged thing, a honey taster, a wanderer in summer gardens.

The final image of Indian art is therefore not even that of the sage, the Buddha figure, but that of Shiva Nataraj, the dancer in time and space. Even if we should penetrate to the center of the temple, we cannot remain there. While life is in us we must live in the world where the Dance is, and to live truly we must join the Dance. There is no reason for this. There is no reason for the world, only rhyme and the rhythm of days and nights, the four seasons without us and within. Life is a Dance and the beginning and the end of our lives are steps only; the Dance goes on with us and without us. In time and space we, as all things, arise and dance and in due time slow and cease to be. The Dance continues. The Dance is; it always *is*.

The Shiva image is not a work of art only; it is a challenge. Shiva Nataraj calls his beholder to awaken from his sleep, to know his true nature as God the dancer, and so to dance. We are asked to abandon ourselves; to suffer the joy and the pain and the pity of things; to stand wide to both the wonder and the wreck of the world, and fearlessly to take part in its turning. In the words of the Carpenter in *Alice*, it is asked of us: "Will you, won't you, will you, won't you, *will* you join the Dance?"

Another Carpenter called similarly:

> *In a manger laid and wrapped I was*
> *So very poor, this was my chance,*
> *Betwixt an ox and a silly poor ass,*
> *To call my true love to the dance.*[2]

Science now assures us that stones dance as surely as stars. A rock is a slow dance; a flower is a little faster. They are equal dances. There are no degrees in the Dance of Life, only differences. The sea advances and retreats. Fish do green dances in the deep. Salmon leap and swallows dip. Tall poplars dance as much as larks and lyrebirds do. The wind makes a dancing girl of the willow and a golden chorus of the wheat. There are many ways of dancing; weird ways and wonderful, strange and simple ways, tender and terrible, innocent and brutal, solemn and bright, muddled and sublime. They are all of the Dance, equally.

Shiva the dancer proclaims that the choice is with us at every moment: to dance with the quick or to join the procession of the dead. The way of the dead brings security, comfort, fame, so that there can be no good reason to join the dance. To give a motive to this way of life, which is the way of love, is to belittle it. The whole point is its pointlessness. One dances for no reason, as the rose opens in the morning and is for no reason red. There is no virtue in it. It is reckless and unreasonable. There is no reward to it. The reason and the reward lie in the dancing; the cause, the aim, the end and the justification of life can lie only in the living of our lives. Life has no meaning, but how much it can mean to be alive! So Shiva asks again and always: "Will you, won't you, will you, won't you, *won't* you join the Dance?"

OPPOSITE. *Shiva Nataraj.* Madras, 13th c. The upper right hand holds a drum that announces the creation of the world; in the upper left is the flame that in time destroys the world. The lower right hand signals "Fear not"; the lower left hand points to the uplifted foot to show freedom from all circumstance. The right foot is on the dwarf, *Ignorance*, who in his place provides a firm footing for the Dance. The face shows calm in the midst of all activity, of the drama of life and death.

If the images of Indian art seem alien to us, it may be because there are parts of ourselves that are alien to us, even alienated from us. If we are shocked by them, it may be because there are bright animals, demons, and dancing gods in us that need to be freed, to be lived with and lived out.

The horror expressed by missionaries and others from the West standing before certain images and temples of India is understandable. The Christian tradition takes up arms against evil and seeks to exclude it. The Hindu tradition encompasses evil, sees it as the corollary and accompaniment of good. When asked why there is evil in the world, Sri Ramana Maharshi replied: "To thicken the plot."

From the first cradle cry to the grave's final quiet, our lives are spent under the sway of opposites. Manifestation implies polarity. From the standpoint of the one, undivided Absolute, the nondual Immensity, this manifest world is therefore illusory. As such, however, it may not only be experienced but should be enjoyed. "Out of joy was the world created," say the Upanishads, "through joy it continues, into joy it returns." When the flowers, the doves, and the rabbits come tumbling out of the magician's hat, we do not bemoan the fact that we are being tricked, that we are subject to illusion. A secondary name for the gods of Hinduism is *krida*, meaning "play." So it is said: "The gods play. The rise, duration, and destruction of the world is their game." The world is created and crowded with apparent contradictions in the way that a child with a smile builds up a castle of sand and with a laugh then tramples it down; so we have life and death, beauty and beast, harvest and hurricane, the serpent and the dove. Indian art must alarm those who believe in a God who is only good, opposed to a Devil who is only bad. God is not good, he is beyond good and evil: he is Good. There are lines by the poet Rainer Maria Rilke: "The fishbone in the throat it suffocates is quite as much at home as in the fish." This will be misunderstood as indifference. The fishbone is *at home*.

LEFT. Detail from *The Demon Horde advancing on the Goddess Chandi Kali*. Guler, 19th c.

All the world's a stage, not in metaphor but in fact. A good play involves both hero and villain, both joy and hazard. We may cheer the hero and hiss the villain, but it is villain and black circumstance that make the adventure and allow its happy ending. We may tremble before these images of the East as we may fear some who inhabit our dreams, but it need only be the fear that a good thriller engenders. One of the hands of these demonic images may lift a severed head, but another will be seen to signal to the beholder with gestures meaning "Peace" and "Fear not." And the tranquil, sad-happy smile of the Buddha image springs from a knowledge of the true nature of the world as theatre, and of the tragicomedy of life. Again there are lines by Rilke, telling how the hero

ABOVE. *The Birth of Evil;* malevolent spirits issuing from Brahma the Creator. Basholi, 18th c.
BELOW. *The Goddess Kali;* Terrible/Divine Mother of the World. Calcutta, 19th c.

Loved his interior world, his interior jungle,
that primal forest within, on whose mute
   overthrownness,
light-green, his heart stood. Loved. Left it,
   continued
out through his own roots into violent beginning
where his tiny birth was already outlived.
   Descended,
lovingly, into the older blood, the ravines where
Frightfulness lurked, still gorged with his fathers.
   And every
terror knew him, and winked, and quite
   understood.
Yes, Horror smiled at him . . .
                              How could he help
loving what smiled at him

We are called by an understanding of Indian art to live what it demonstrates: a life lived abundantly *here*, in awareness of Eternity *now*. This is not done by keeping the world at a distance, but by delighting in it. This is not shallow folly but Wisdom, the way of Sophia, the consort of God, possessed by the Lord "in the beginning of his way. . . . And I was daily his delight, rejoicing always before him; rejoicing in his habitable earth; and my delight was with the sons of men." Aware of the one undying impulse in us all, we may be quick then to embrace its many mortalities, giving ourselves not to such abstractions as "God is love," but to the actual love of God in the guise of a girl, a boy, a wife, a husband, each beast, flower, rock and puddle, every creature and thing. Living in this way, loving in this way, we may know again, as we knew in the days of our child-

ABOVE. *Radha and Krishna in the grove*. Kangra, 18th c.
OPPOSITE. Nihal Chand : *Radha*. Kishangarh, 18th c.

hood, not in the mind apart but in whole and hale and happy being, we may know wonder again and the wonder of all things, bitter as sweet: a storm, a still pond, a singing bird, a stalking cat, a hare in the moonlight, bread and wine, a husband and wife in bed, a child in a cradle, our own awakened selves, God. The world in this way no longer proves to be opaque, as to the materialist, nor yet transparent, as to the idealist; it is a translucent world with the shine not only on and around all things, but also in them, a "country of lit-upness," a landscape transfigured by the love of it, a world made real by the grace of our being in it wholly.

34

Religion strives. Art celebrates. The images of Indian art tell that the longing soul and the laggard body are not two things, as religion and sex are not two things. Sex is not a genital itch of some sixty years' duration, but our total response all our life long to all that lies about us. There is no love that is sacred. There is no love that is profane. Simply, there is love.

And God is love, as the Christians claim, but this love is whole and not of spirit or body or mind or soul alone, for we are not these things only. These are but aspects and appearances of one Whole that cannot be distinguished or divided. The "Pure Love" of St. Catherine of Siena is what brings a man to a woman, a stallion to a mare, stag to doe, ram to ewe, the toad to his warty lady, even proton to electron. That love which, in Dante's phrase, "moves the sun and the other stars" is also the reason for the many rabbits in the world.

Indian art as well assents to the Christian statement that the Kingdom of Heaven lies within us; within us and all about us, if we will have eyes to see. Heaven is here and now. Eden is everywhere. Each man is Adam; each woman, Eve. Every man in his inmost is the blue god, Krishna, and every woman is Radha, radiant. And the valley of Vrindavana is not a mythical place nor only a painted one; it is not in an India far away and long ago; it is here and now. If we would cease to seek; if we would be still and *see*—the Garden is all about us, the hallowed place is here. Another name for it is that of the town or village, hill or valley where we walk. The poet Yeats once asked:

*Do our woods and winds and ponds
Cover more quiet woods, more shining winds,
    more star-glimmering ponds?*

They do. They are the woods, the winds and ponds we see and do not see. The quiet, the shine, and the glimmering are here for the seeing. It is the same tree that the fool and the sage both see—the difference in being is a difference in seeing.

Yeats also asked: *Is Eden out of time and out of space?* It is. Out of time and out of space, in the eternity of our everyday and everywhere, here and now. *Iti! Iti!* insisted the old Indian: It is here! It is here!

37

REFERENCES

1. G. K. CHESTERTON
2. ANON. From a poem, "My Dancing Day," known since the seventeenth century
3. RAINER MARIA RILKE : *Duino Elegies,* translated by J. B. Leishman and Stephen Spender

The Way of Emptiness

ABOVE. Drawing from *The Mustard Seed Garden Manual of Painting*. 17th c.

40

2 The Way of Emptiness

We are the children of this beautiful planet that we have lately seen photographed from the moon. We were not delivered into it by some god, but have come forth from it. We are its eyes and mind, its seeing and its thinking. And the earth, together with the sun, this light around which it flies like a moth, came forth, we are told, from a nebula; and that nebula, in turn, from space. So that we are the mind, ultimately, of space . . . each in his own way at one with all, and with no horizons.

JOSEPH CAMPBELL

Space, vast space, is the friend of being.
GASTON BACHELARD

AN OLD AND PERSISTENT DREAM has haunted the heart and mind of man. It has been given the many names of Eden, of Paradise, of Atlantis, the Garden of the Hesperides, Zion, the Land of Beulah, the Abode of Bliss. Whatever the name, it is of the same essential nature—a place of light and ease where man walks not only on the earth but *of* it, even as the soaring lark, the stalking tiger, as any wild flower in the woods. In contrast to man's severed, isolated self, bird and beast, fish and flower can seem all of a piece with the earth, with its wild and its kindly elements, and so at peace with themselves and all that befalls them of sun and shadow, increase and death.*

In search of the meaning of that dream and of the means to realize it in his own day, a man of the West may well turn to his traditional religion, only to find that it puts his fulfillment outside the natural order of things, beyond the world as he knows it, in some other Reality, elsewhere: God above, apart and wholly Other, created light, the heavenly bodies, earth and all its creatures; he then made Adam and, as an afterthought, Eve. All was made to minister to man, who though fashioned of the clay of the earth was also essentially other, made in the image of that supernatural, supermanly God.

"A culture sustained by a faith in a personal God cannot find reality in Nature."[1] We may no longer believe, but can still suffer the first chapter of Genesis. Centuries after Copernicus, the Universe still turns about the mind of Western man. In spite of Darwin, we do not *feel* ourselves of one family with all other forms of nature. That first separation of God from man, and man from nature, shows now in our ashen skies, in ravaged hills, felled woods and stinking rivers, in all the small deaths and great losses that have followed on man's dominion.

*A recently translated Dead Sea Scroll records a disciple asking Jesus: "Master, how can we get into the Kingdom of Heaven?" Jesus answers: "Follow the birds, the beasts, the fish, and they will lead you in."

OPPOSITE. Ma Lin : *Scholar reclining and watching rising clouds.* 13th c.

41

If we cannot now find reality in Nature, we are lost. The "conquest of nature" is the defeat of man as of all else. It is not a matter of knowledge. We well know the interdependence of all things, and we use this knowledge to further new destruction. Without a deeply felt realization of the Universe as one body, we cannot know the part that is man, and so the part he needs to play.

This necessary vision of the one body of the Universe for lack of which we may well perish is not offered by religion in the West. Our science, however, comes to tell of it and so surprisingly confirms the insights of ancient cultures that we have named primitive and heathen.

An old Chinese text that modern physics would not fault proclaims: *"There is no Creator. Everything produces itself and is not produced by others. This is the natural way of the Universe."* There is no accepted creation myth in China, but a popular folk legend offers a clue to old Chinese attitudes: Once was Chaos, like an egg, enormous and everywhere, not created but simply existent, with nothing outside or apart from it. Chaos opened up to form the earth, the sky, and original Man. He grew to fill the space between earth and sky, then died, and his breath became wind, his voice thunder, his body the mountain ranges of the earth, his blood its rivers, his flesh its soil, his sweat the sweet rain, while the fleas upon him became man and woman. Fleas in old China went with a body inevitably, so that men and women were seen to be a part of the one body of Nature.

Nature, not man, was the measure of things, and all things were true insofar as they were true to Nature, playing their part in the whole. The very Emperor was subject to the same natural laws as the least of things. As head of the social body, he had it in him to bring plenty or famine to his people; his follies could overwhelm the world, his lechery give birth to plague. When the Yellow River burst its banks, something was wrong because somebody was wrong. The good Emperor, however, brought only good about; the earth answered to the way of a wise and *natural* man: crops grew high,

fruit ripened, children fattened, naturally and inevitably. It was not so much a matter of ruling well as of being well. *"The way to do is to be."*[2] The true Emperor ruled as the sun, by radiance, not by will and intention but as a simple consequence of his own true nature. This followed upon the fact that the nature of the Emperor was that of the Universe and of all that composed it. In all beings of earth and sky and underworld was the one Nature. It came to be known as the Tao. With its roots reaching back into the dark of China's beginning, the conception of the Tao had its flowering in the five thousand characters set down by Lao Tsu as the *Tao Te Ching,* and had fruit a while later in the laughter of Chuang Tsu.

The *Tao Te Ching* tells of a way of life that can be lived lightly in spite of all pain and harrowing, in kinship with all else that is wild and alone and at home in the Universe, on the move always while always deeply rooted in an indefinable sense of *Something* that is no thing, and so beyond the threat of warring men. Paradoxically, it may at first seem, an awareness of this No-thing—called Emptiness here—is accompanied by a delight in all things as transitory and vulnerable as oneself. It is far from the immortal abstractions that infect men's minds and twist their essential natures—all ideals, politics, philosophies, religions. The concern of the *Tao Te Ching* is with what *is,* when it naturally is; with man when he is so, naturally; when he is empty, that is, of all wish and insistent will to have things otherwise, knowing well that the world, for good or ill, takes shape from himself. "If the empty places are right," said a Chinese painter, "the whole body is alive." Emptiness sets a man square upon the earth and smiling.

OPPOSITE. Fu Pao-shih : *Diamond Cliffs.* 20th c.

The *Tao* of Lao Tsu has been understood as *Godhead,* as *Logos,* as *Universal Spirit,* as *The Supreme Oneness,* as *Elan Vital,* as *Existence,* as *Nature.* It is understood here as all that these names can imply, and as no one of them. The *Tao* is most frequently translated as the *Way,* but it is not a way that leads anywhere; there is nowhere to go, and no need. It is the way of things, the way things *are.*

"I do not know its name," said Lao Tsu. *"I call it Tao."*

It is called here by one of its aspects: *Emptiness.* It is empty of all concepts, all qualities—even that of emptiness. Calling it Emptiness calls it out of antiquity, for Emptiness is now and everywhere; it is the nature of Nature, and so of every man and woman, beast, bird, insect, and plant, of hill and valley, cloud and stream, sea and sky.

It is called Emptiness here, but it could as easily be called Fullness, since it is the ground, surround, and being of all the ten thousand things. Each and every thing arises out of Emptiness as the hiss of the adder arises out of Silence, and the breast of the robin is Invisibility's bright appearance. Emptiness does not create the many things, it reveals them by showing itself as them. It is not the sum of things, but is each thing wholly and only and always for the little while that each thing is—one russet leaf is autumn, a green leaf is spring. All things are One and that is No-thing. Call it Tao. Call it Emptiness. Call it Fullness. Call it any one of the ten thousand things. Call it Toad.

"Once the whole is divided the parts need names." Call it by your own name then, it is who you *are.* Call it any one. No name is nearer than another and no one further. Call it anything. Better, do not call it; "nearer than hands or feet," it needs no calling. It does not come or go; it remains to be *seen.*

"The Tao is invisible—it is beyond all form." But look! yellow leaves on the lawn! *"The Tao is inaudible—it is beyond all sound."* But listen! the storm and the missel thrush singing! *"The Tao is no thing, but you will not find it apart from things."* It is the Nature of all things—the circling of the seasons, the drifting of the stars and the moon's curving, falling of water and fire burning, hooting owl and screaming mouse, scenting honeysuckle and stinging nettle. It is the way of a man when he walks or digs or does nothing, aware of what he does and does not do; the way of a woman when she sews with awareness or kneads her bread so or sits still by a fire. It is all that a man does when he acts naturally, in accordance with his true nature, undistracted, empty of dreams, *aware.* Desire destroys. Aversion blinds. Seeking divides and severs us. To seek anything is to make an object of it, and so to make a subject of oneself, separate and apart. Wanting any one thing tears the world in two. What we lack is nothing we can look for. We lack *looking,* simply. "This world, in so far as it is quite empty of God, is God himself. . . . The imagination is continually at work filling up the fissures through which grace might pass. Grace fills empty spaces but it can only enter where there is a void to receive it, and it is grace itself which makes this void. If we can accept no matter what void, what stroke of fate can prevent us from loving the universe?"[3]

OPPOSITE. *Frog.* Sung, 10th–13th c.

寶樹具妙相香界圖一林大葉若壞衲紛披
何蕭森林中僧獣歸誰向石塢尋持此念佛
鳥清畫連夕陰　　　　　佛弟子金農圖

Tao is everywhere, is everything. "Surely the Lord is in this place and I knew him not." To trust in the Lord is to let him be, to know nothing of him, to attend to the task at hand and put the kettle on to boil. "Closer is He than breathing; nearer than hands and feet." What then can be done to bring God about? What needs to be done? Pour water on the tea leaves, be still and wait. The desire for God is the denial of him. Fill the cup and drink. Reality may not be sought, only found, and it is found in drinking, tasting, hearing, touching, smelling, seeing. The godly know nothing of God. The wise know nothing of wisdom; they sip their tea seemingly as fools do. We are fools only because we do not know what we do. Full of thought, we are blindfolded. Emptiness is awareness.

Seeking God we are with wide eyes seeking sight, "riding on an ox looking for an ox to ride." The Tao is not to be looked for; it is *looking*; it is consciousness; it is what we are. *"To seek after Tao is like turning round in circles to see one's own eyes. Those who understand this walk on."*

All is given. We have but to see and receive it; not to reach out but to recognize, to realize our Emptiness. In Emptiness there is nothing lacking, for there is no one. "The marvelous nature of the ordinary person is fundamentally empty and has no fixed character. Such is the truly skylike quality of one's natural self. . . . The emptiness of universal space can contain the mountains and rivers, the great earth with its springs, streams and waterfalls, grass, trees and dense forests, its sinners and saints, and the ways of good and evil. . . . All these are in the void, and the ordinary person's nature is void in just this way."

So Hui-neng told it. Te-shan also said it:

With no thing in mind and no mind in things— vacant and spirited, empty and marvelous!

So did Sodo:

> *In my hut this spring,*
> *there is nothing . . .*
> *There is everything!*

LEFT. Chin Nung : *Monk under a palm tree.* 17th–18th c.

野風空水面吕連折溪灣野鳥碧空下蒼紅乧照開
造僊壇落賣涌到閒新出一庭月榮門夜未關
洪崖山歌

ABOVE. Huang Shen : Hut in the wilderness. Album leaf, 18th c.

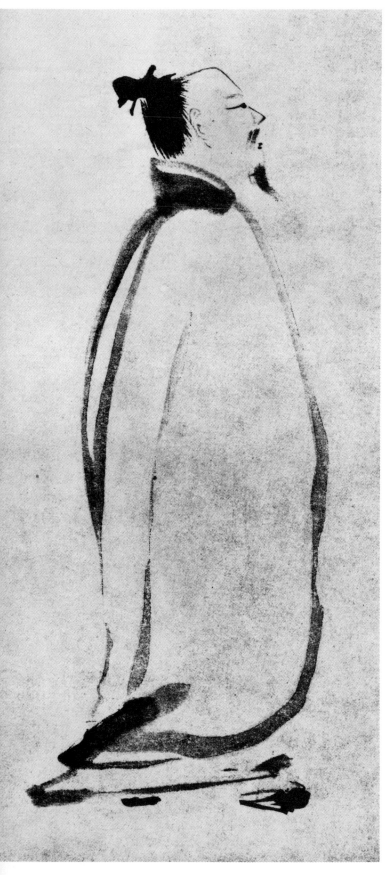

To be void and skylike, to be vacant and spirited, empty and marvelous, to have nothing and so to have everything—these will seem impossible paradoxes to many in the West. The very thought of Emptiness can fill us with dread. Pascal confessed: "The eternal silence of these infinite spaces terrifies me."

It can come upon any man at any time he cares to be silent, dares to be still: "All you have to do is to pause for a moment in your work and ask yourself: Why am I doing this? What is it all for? Did I come into the world supplied with a soul which may very likely be immortal, for the sole purpose of sitting every day at this desk? Ask yourself these questions thoughtfully, seriously. Reflect even for a moment on their significance—and I guarantee that, firmly seated though you may be in your hard or padded chair, you will feel at once that the void has opened beneath you, that you are sliding headlong, fast and faster, into nothingness."[4]

Understandably, we seldom pause to ask such questions but work on, and when work is done, we arm ourselves against the empty hours by activity of any and every kind—good times or good deeds. Society provides for one, religion approves the other; both share the same certainty: idleness is the very devil; it invites Emptiness.

But there are those among us, artists of one kind or another, whose activity involves a measure of idleness, for whom Emptiness is a creative condition: "Amongst the greatest things which are to be found among us, the Being of Nothingness is the greatest," said Leonardo da Vinci with all the assurance of an age that could believe that, whatever else, man was not nothing.

We are less sure today. We have come to know the murk that underlies the shine of our moral selves, the rot that gives birth to high ideals; we have learned—it is hoped—the lie of progress, the hollowness of all political and religious persuasions. We have for so long been assured of the nobility of man made in the image of God, "how like an angel" . . . and we have seen the charred bodies of Hiroshima, of Belsen, Buchenwald, and Vietnam. Evidence of man's "special place in creation" lies all about us in foul air and the stench of rivers, in the bloodshed of innocent beasts, in factory farms and pesticides. The press of a button now can bring the world to an end. Nothingness is near at hand.

Staring into the mass graves of our hopes for man, of all old beliefs, dreams, and ideals, we can also seem near to Nothingness, for we are shorn even of that sense of tragedy that has been the support of religion, as of so much poetry and of all forms of art. "I speak of an art weary of its puny exploits, weary of pretending to be able, of being able. . . . If only I could speak and say Nothing, really Nothing."[5]

Our arts mirror us, but even the best of art stops at Nothing. Nothingness is not Emptiness; it is only the extremity of things, the farthest edge of all that we have known and have found wanting. Emptiness is unknown, unknowable, and beyond want. Wanting to say Nothing is still something, still wanting. In Emptiness there can be no wish to speak and it is for this reason that even poets falter. So Rainer Maria Rilke sighed:

We've never, no not for a single day
pure space before us, such as that which flowers
endlessly open into: always world
and never nowhere without no: that pure
unsuperintended element one breathes
endlessly knows and never craves.[6]

But Rilke stayed on the edge, it seems, and did not take the next step into pure space, for that would have meant an end to sighing, even an end to poetry as he knew it, certainly an end to the Poet. There are no words in Space to tell of it, so that poets may be withheld by the wish to be poets. At most a man may come out of the experience stammering as Blaise Pascal— earlier in his life he had confessed that contemplation of the "silence of the infinite spaces" terrified him; when later he was to enter Space and experience it, he scribbled those words found after his death on a scrap of paper sewn into his doublet:

From about half past ten in the evening
until about half past twelve, midnight
  F I R E
God of Abraham, God of Isaac, God of Jacob

Not of the philosophers and scholars.
Certainty, Certainty. Feeling. Joy. Peace.
Joy, joy, joy, tears of joy.

"The mind in creation is a fading coal." Pascal wrote *F I R E* at the start, but then fell back upon the language of theologians, upon old ways of thought: "*I have fled him, renounced him, crucified him. May I never be separated again. My God, do you forsake me? . . . He saves himself only by ways taught in the Bible. Total submission to Jesus Christ and to my Director. I will not forget your teachings, Amen.*" Eckhart, too, in telling of Space, could use only the words and concepts available at the time, though he strained them beyond all recognition in speaking of "that still desert of the Godhead—as void as though it were not—where there never was seen difference, neither Father, Son, nor Holy Ghost, where there is no one at home"—making such seeming nonsense of the old hallowed names that he was condemned as a heretic.

Today, however, there are those who can more easily read beyond his words to his meaning; for them the old gods have proved unreal and they would rather have nothing than hold to what seems false. "Nothingness might save or destroy those who face it, but those who ignore it are condemned to unreality."[7]

OPPOSITE. Liang K'ai : *The poet Li Po* (detail). 13th c.

In place of the old fables we have called for facts and have looked to science for them. Rejecting all the old ways of religion, science not long ago asserted a material universe. The nature of things was to be discovered in time by empirical material means. With heads unbowed, with unshielded eyes and minds unclouded by vapid dreams of God the Father, Son, and Holy Ghost, of angelic hosts in a faraway and future Heaven, we could walk with the aid only of objective science, firm footed upon a solid earth.

But science itself now takes the ground from under our feet. We are now told that *"that which is is a shell floating in the infinitude of that which is not"*[8] . . . The Universe is as the surface of a soap bubble, *"and the substance out of which this bubble is blown, the soap film, is empty space welded onto empty time."*[9] . . . *"In space there are no directions and no boundaries; without things occupying it, it is nothing."*[10] . . . *"Matter is a convenient formula for describing what happens where it isn't."*[11] . . . *"All galaxies, stars, planets, and human beings are manifestations of disturbances in a tenuous sea. They are waves, streams, ripples, flurries in a ceaseless change."*[12]

"Our logic," said Bergson, "born of solids, is a logic of solids." What then can be logically said of the shadowy world we inhabit? *"The frank realisation that physical science is concerned with a world of shadows is one of the most significant advances."*[13] . . . *"In the last analysis, the material world fades and yields to a round of unreal phantoms; the final substance of nature, far from being substance, is only a complicated disguise."*[14]

. . . *"The stuff of the world is mind stuff; by 'mind' I do not exactly mean 'mind' and by 'stuff' I do not at all mean 'stuff.'"*[15]

Out of the mouths of the most respected scientists come statements that offend all common sense*—particles may also be waves all the while and may be "everywhere at once"; they are "disembodied spins." Elementary particles may be composed of yet more elementary particles called "Quarks" (with acknowledgment to James Joyce's *Finnegans Wake*), and one theory has been named the Eightfold Way (with a bow to the Buddha). "Strangeness" is now a technical term to describe the behavior

*In the popular imagination men of science appear as sober ice-cold logicians, electronic brains mounted on dry sticks. But if one were shown on anthology of typical extracts from their letters and autobiographies with no names mentioned, and then asked to guess their profession, the likeliest answer would be: a bunch of poets or musicians of a rather romantically naïve kind. ARTHUR KOESTLER : *The Act of Creation*

of particles. Time may be reversed, all rules violated, at any moment unexpected things may happen. We expected firm and certain principles from science, and we are given the Principle of Uncertainty. The statements grow increasingly surrealistic: we learn of "negative mass," of "holes in space," of time flowing backward. The solid world that science once promised is but a wave. A wave is movement. What moves? "Short of calling it the grin of the Cheshire Cat, it was named 'psi field' or 'psi function.'"[16]

Science now leads us through the Looking Glass and says it is no dream; nor are we in Wonderland only, we are *of* it. All that is told of the Universe is told of us, as of every one of the ten thousand things. Insofar as we are at all, we are wavicles and space, overwhelmingly the latter. Joliot-Curie tells that all the nuclei of atoms that go to make up the mass of an average man, if packed like grain in a sack, would seem as a single speck of dust to be seen only when sunlight beams into a dark room.

> *Golden lads and girls all must*
> *As chimney-sweepers come to dust.*[17]

And that dust comes to nothing.

But if it comes to nothing, it also comes from nothing. Material is *"created out of nothing; it must be supposed that there is literally a true creation going on as a continuous process."*[18] Golden lads and girls, all shining beasts and birds of paradise, armadillos and ruby-bottomed apes, lumbering elephants and leaping fleas, sloths and flying squirrels, sharks and seahorses, dragonflies and centipedes, the lotus, the rose and corn-on-the-cob, all the ten thousand things arise out of nothing we can know and nowhere we can name. So the scientist also stops at nothing; seems now to stand on the edge of all that is known and even knowable: *"Something unknown is doing we know not what."*[19]

OPPOSITE. "Horse-head" nebula in the constellation Orion.
RIGHT. "Cone" nebula in the constellation Monocerus.

Science stops at Nothing, necessarily, for to go beyond is to cease to be scientific only. The objectivity that has guided science and has made possible all its findings, achievements, and its many gifts to us now stands in the way.

Looking objectively at the Universe and all the many things, the scientist sees a Unity that must include himself, the subject. "The physicist himself who describes the world is in his own account, himself constructed of it. He is, in short, made of a conglomeration of the very particles he describes, no more, no less, bound together and obeying such general laws as he himself has managed to find and to record. Thus we cannot escape the fact that the world as we know it is constructed in order (and thus in such a way as to be able) to see itself. This is indeed amazing. Not so much in view of what it sees, although this may appear fantastic enough, but in respect of the fact that it sees at all. But *in order* to do so, evidently it must first cut itself up into at least one state which sees, and at least one other state which is seen. In this severed and mutilated condition, whatever it sees is *only partially* itself. . . . Thus the world, wherever it appears as a physical universe, must always seem to us, its representatives, to be playing a kind of hide-and-seek with itself . . . the universe must expand to escape the telescopes through which we, who are it, are trying to capture it, which is us. The snake eats itself, the dog chases its tail."[20]

The snake is Orobouros, primal dragon of the beginning; with its tail in its mouth it makes a circle, the symbol of wholeness, the sign of unity. It is the shape of zero, that absence of number that makes possible all numerical play. It is not nothing, for that is only and always the opposite of something. Nothing, by definition, cannot give rise to something. Beyond and at back of all opposites lies Emptiness, and it is this that reveals the ten thousand things to the scientist who is of the same Emptiness. Science tells that all living

organisms move in space not by progression but by quantum jumps. The scientist, if he is not to remain as of old in the mere knowledge of things, must similarly jump.

And so it is with all men. There can be no reason to jump. Reasoning is remaining. There can only be reasons to remain with all that is old and known and secure underfoot. "Logically, when one comes to an empty space, one ought to halt. But life is that which leaps."[21] To step into Space is to let go of all that has hitherto upheld us; it is to fall, even, it seems, to die.

So it must seem while we stand fearfully on the edge. It is a fearful step all the while we do not take it. In Space there is no fear, for there is nothing to fear, and no one.

Words can make no sense of it, but in rare moments we know what it is to be no one. Sometimes, in spite of ourselves, we are lifted into Space; in such moments we have hints of Emptiness that can haunt us always. It may be explained as "a sudden feeling of contact with a

ABOVE. Attributed to Kuo Hsi : *Clearing autumn skies over mists and valleys* (detail). 11th c.

unity more real than the apparent complexity of things . . . not when seeking to escape the visible world, but rather when that world was seeming to them most sublimely real."[22] But it is nothing that can be so clearly told, nothing that can be named or known or recognized. Indeed it is nothing at all, and yet . . .

It can happen anywhere; at any time we can be startled out of ourselves by anything seen or heard or somehow sensed as never before—the drip of a tap may do it, or sunlight on broken glass, a scribble on a wall may do it, a scent, a rook in an autumn sky, a curlew's cry, the eyes of a stranger in the street. "Quick now, here, now, always—"

53

There are also hints and hauntings everywhere in the work of those with eyes to see and the means to tell, the poets and artists among us. Among these, none have pointed so clearly as those painters of landscape and of small forms of life in China eight centuries ago, for whom Emptiness was the element in which they lived and moved and had being, as salmon in a river, as hawks in the sky.

What other cultures have sought by way of religion, philosophy, or science, China has found by way of painting. Artists of the Sung period found in landscape painting a language that could suggest the one Reality that informs and irradiates the ten thousand things. Reality cannot be told, cannot be imagined, but such landscapes are pointings to it, even echoes of it. The ambiguity and bewilderment of words are replaced by mountains and rivers, rocks and trees; the disturbance of thought gives way to silence and still seeing. "Only those who are quiet can understand," said the painter Chang Keng. Quiet puts one within the painting, moving along the way that leads among those high mountains, beside those rivers, trees, rocks; one moves, that is, in the way these things move, in the way of all things, "still and still moving," the way things *are*, the way one *is*.*

*Shut your eyes, wait, think of nothing. Now, open them. . . . One sees nothing but a great colored undulation. What then? An irradiation and glory of color. That is what a picture should give us, a warm harmony, an abyss in which the eye is lost, a secret germination, a colored state of grace. All these tones circulate in the blood, don't they? One is revivified, born into the real world, one finds oneself, one becomes the painting. To love a painting, one must first have drunk deeply of it in long draughts. Lose consciousness. Descend with the painter into the dim tangled roots of things, or rise again from them in colors, be steeped in the light of them. PAUL CEZANNE

To look upon such paintings as objects is to remain a subject, separate and apart. One who looks *at* a painting is not *looking*. In looking there is no one. Looking is a state of Emptiness, as *listening* is. To listen to the words of sages is but to listen to the words of sages. All words fall from grace, but by way of words, the sage points beyond them, as the painter in drawing the line somewhere on a blank stretch of silk, draws attention to what is nowhere, being at once everywhere and "always-so." Words are of things. The sage tells of No-thing. Truly listening, we *are* Nothing.

So to *look* is to lose oneself: observer and observed are One and that One reaches beyond the space that contains them to the unending Universe. A Sung painting is never completed; it was not done once and forever some eight centuries ago; it is not an object but a process that was before the painter was, before he put a hand to it; it continues and includes the observer who stands before it in his time here and now, goes beyond him, and reaches out of time.

Seeing man as the measure of all things, the Western mind can feel lost before Chinese paintings that seem to have little or no place for him. It is not so: man is there in his place among all other things, and true to scale. He is also *here*, standing before the painting now, being, if he truly looks, a part of that painting that has no confining frame. There are no "still lifes" in Sung paintings, no cut flowers in a vase, only the tip of a branch perhaps that reaches out of the paper to have root in the space of the room in which it is seen. The mountains range to left and right, the river flows beyond the silk, the clouds sail out of it over the head of the observer into the sky and space that contains the room, the house, the street, the city, the country, the earth, the very universe. Entering a Sung painting, a man may find his place in the universe.

OPPOSITE AND RIGHT. Tao-chi : Details from *The Waterfall on Mount Lu*. 17th–18th c.

"The finest landscapes," said Kuo Hsi, "are those one can wander in, those one can live in." It is not a matter of form only, and not of spirit only, for these are not to be separated. "The Chinese painter may spend years in wandering among the hills and streams so that this natural order, which is but a visible manifestation of the cosmic order, may reveal itself to him. But how can he express the intensity of the awareness that comes to him in these

moments of spiritual revelation before the ultimate mysteries of the universe? The language of metaphysics is too remote, too abstract, to convey an experience that, while partly psychic, is also intensely visual. For the wanderer in the mountains attains awareness through no mere feat of imagination, but through a journey in space and time, in a real landscape. Bare rock and green foliage, heat and cold, light and shadow, sound and silence—these belong not to a world of the philosophers and metaphysicians but to a world in which visual and psychic experiences are inextricably interwoven. Such experiences can find expression only in a language that is both visual and abstract—visual enough so that the forms that give rise to it may be apprehended, conveyed, and recognized for what they are, yet abstract enough to convey upon the forms thus created the validity of a general, eternal truth."[23]

The Tao cannot be told, it cannot be painted. Being invisible, it could seem that the only fitting representation is a blank sheet of paper, but blankness of this kind in no way conveys the way of Tao, the wonder of Emptiness, nor suggests it as the source and being of all the ten thousand things. But when a master painter takes the empty paper and makes a mark in one corner only, the whole sheet becomes alive; what was only blank is now vibrant, potent, pregnant.

This is the "mystery of Emptiness" of which the Sung painters spoke. By way of what is painted, what cannot be painted is implied—the invisible Reality, the Tao, is suggested. Let a master brush a small bird upon a blank sheet and blankness becomes the wide upholding sky; what was only empty becomes Emptiness, all heaven is immediately at hand. Drawing a bird, he creates a sky for the bird to fly in. If there were no bird, there would be no sky. Without the sky the bird could not fly, could not *be*. Without Emptiness nothing could *be*; with Emptiness all comes into being.

To reveal the invisible that in turn gives meaning to the visible is not a matter of marking a blank sheet; it is a matter of Emptiness, of the mark of a master, a man of Emptiness. It is not simply or even necessarily a matter of skill, not a matter of doing, but of *being*.

"The way to do is to be," said Lao Tsu. The way to paint is to be—to be Empty, that is. "When I begin to paint," said a Chinese artist, "I do not know that I am painting. I entirely forget that it is myself who holds the brush."*

In the act of painting there is no painter. Bird and blossom, tree, mountain and river are not the outcome of any willed action but simply of reflecting. The mind of the painter, as that of the sage, is compared to a mirror. When a man allows the busy surface of his mind to settle, it is as though he ceased to disturb the surface of a lake, which then, naturally and inevitably, reflects the sky, the bird or cloud or whatsoever happens to be there, and reflects them without any distortion, as they *are*.

*I have a terrible lucidity at moments, these days when nature is so beautiful. I am not conscious of myself any more and the picture comes to me as in a dream. VINCENT VAN GOGH

BELOW. Kao Feng-han : *Flower painting*. 17th–18th c.

There is a verse of twelve hundred years ago:

Wild geese fly across the sky.
Their image is reflected on the water.
The geese do not mean to cast their image on the
*   water.*
The water has no mind to hold the image of the
*   geese.* [24]

The water is still. The geese go over. The image appears. Nothing is "done"; it happens without intention, without will or striving, naturally and inevitably. So it is with the painting of a master who has come upon stillness, whose mind and heart are empty, as with a mirror. The image appears, and because it is not distorted by the painter's mind, it is truly reflected, its nature is revealed. Since the true nature of any one thing is the Nature of all, a painting of a goose can reveal the Tao; goose and "God" are one.

To imply that such paintings are "religious" is to have many in the West searching for evidence of it. They look for saints and find running streams, for holy men and find craggy mountains, curling mists; they seek angels and all the appurtenances of Paradise and find a toad, a crane, an ape on a branch, a sprig of plum blossom, a single bamboo.

ABOVE. Hui-Tsung : *Quail and iris*. 11th–12th c.

59

An artist in the West intending a religious painting will start upon a supernatural subject, a religious object. He turns from the findings of his everyday to suggest another world than this one. He paints an Ascension perhaps, or a Virgin Mother, a choir of Angels, Cherubim and Seraphim—extraordinary beings, all without sweat on their brows and so unknown to us in this world. Such paintings must point to the absence of God. All religious art, as we ordinarily know it, as all recognized spiritual activity, shows a lack of faith, a want of that frail yet abiding sense of that actual presence we have called God, and some call Tao. The strength of our belief in God is the measure of our lack of him. A man whose body is browned by the sun does not believe in it. He sits and sweats and casts a shadow, sips his tea, listens to the blackbird, looks to the hills and smiles when the sun seems to go down behind them, knowing well that it is only seeming; the sun *is* and is "always-so." So the sun-brown painter does not paint the sun but any part of the sunlit world he happens to see—a hill, a pond, an apple perhaps, and it is by the light upon the apple that we are made aware of the sun. One cannot paint light, only the things upon which it lights—the ten thousand lighted things. The man of Tao, when he paints, does not try to paint the Tao but any one of the ten thousand things that reveals it.

So it is that a Christ is in no way suggested by the agony and complexity of a crucifixion scene; this only reflects the agonized complexity of the Christian painter's mind. There is, however, a bamboo painting that shows Jesus the Christ, simply and unequivocally. The bamboo is empty, as he of all self-centeredness; it bends to the wind, "resists not evil," and always rights itself. It is a thing of extraordinary strength and infinite grace. Such a bamboo can suggest the being of a Jesus, the true nature of him, which is the Nature of all things.

OPPOSITE. *Bamboo*. ca. 14th c.

61

There is but one Nature: Jesus and the earth he walked on are one with us all. Astronomy now tells it: "The Universe is everything: both living and inanimate things, both atoms and galaxies, and if the spiritual exists as well as the material, of spiritual things also, and if there is a Heaven and Hell, of Heaven and Hell too; for by its very nature the Universe is the totality of all things."[25]

Oneness is a matter of fact, but one cannot know Oneness, for oneself and Oneness are two things. One cannot know Emptiness, for Emptiness knows no one. One cannot experience the Tao, for one is it; because of it, one can be at ease, laughing or weeping, walking or sitting, lazing or making music, a painting, a pot of tea, a bread loaf, love. "The world of Emptiness is not some world without crying and without laughing. Emptiness in the tears themselves, Emptiness in the smiles themselves—this is the real Emptiness."[26] If Emptiness is not in and all about all our acts and occasions, they are out of context, we miss the whole point of them.

So we miss the point of a bamboo painting if we see it only as the painting of a bamboo in the manner of a Western "still life." The painter's point, however, is also missed if we do *not* see it as a painting of a bamboo simply, if we strive to see beyond the bamboo, seeking meaning in it, understanding it only as a symbol of something else, as God, or Tao, or Whatever.

The painter paints the form of the bamboo. That is all he can paint, but if he is in touch with the nature of the bamboo, Nature is revealed. So his bamboo is a bamboo, and yet. . . . That "and yet . . . ," the indefinable "something" that hovers about and inhabits a great painting is what haunts us. It may be a painting that makes us so wondering and still; it may be a pot, the form of a book, an old cobbler's bench, anything "men have made with wakened hands and breathed soft life into."[27] What haunts us is the life that shows, the *suchness*, the *isness* of the thing, the *Tao* of it.

"I lift up my finger and the whole universe comes along with it."[28] The painting of any ordinary everyday thing can reveal the Whole that it is.

It will to those who are empty and so have eyes to see. To paint a bamboo the painter must "empty the mind and heart" and so come upon the nature of the bamboo. To come upon the nature of the bamboo painting, to *see* it, we must be similarly empty. To *see* is Emptiness. Emptiness is Tao. In this way a painting can bring Emptiness about. So Chinese painters have been called sages and magicians: their paintings are not for entertainment or pleasure only; they are potent, magical, they bring wonders about, reveal the Tao. "When one approaches the wonderful," said Hui Tsung, "one knows not whether art is Tao or Tao is art."*

*You see I have made a great discovery: I no longer believe in anything. Objects don't exist for me except in so far as a *rapport* exists between them, and between them and myself. When one attains this harmony, one reaches a sort of intellectual non-existence—what I can only describe as a state of peace—which makes everything possible and right. Life then becomes a perpetual revelation. *Ça, c'est la vraie poésie!* GEORGES BRAQUE, in *The Observer*, London, 1 December 1937

OPPOSITE. *Bamboo in moonlight.* 16th c.

To wander in Chinese landscape paintings is to be unburdened by thought, to be rid of that disease of dualism that infects the religious views of the world, dividing God from man, man from nature, spirit from matter.

The old Chinese view well understood that the manifest world is under the sway of natural opposites: male and female, light and dark, youth and age, life and death. These and all their like do not conflict but complement one another to make a whole. The way of Tao is the way of man and woman; the marriage of opposites gives birth to all the ten thousand things, each one playing its part in accordance with its own nature. There is no division between natural opposites, only differences, and it is these differences that make for the delight and the one dance of things. Being true to their own opposing natures, all opposites are of one Nature.

Looking at the things of heaven and earth
One finds the one spirit in all transformations.
This moving power influences in a mysterious way
all objects and gives them their natures.
No one can say what it is, but it is something
  natural. [29]

The one spirit, the Tao, is moving and it is natural. In this it contrasts with those concepts of Reality assumed by the many religions: Jehovah, God, and Allah are images of a Supreme Being, above and beyond the natural world, immovable, unmanifest, apart. The Hindu Brahman is also still and other.

In the light of such images of Being, our lives in this world of becoming must seem shadowy and in varying degree unreal, for we are ourselves said to be made in the image of such Being.

But if any man comes to care for the truth of things, he must start where he stands and with what he is. Putting aside all that we have been told, leaving aside religion and all manner of make-believe, we are faced with the fact of things as they are for us. Whatever else they may be, all things are clearly fragile and transitory; from their first birth to the last death of their lives, they are forever changing, there is no still being in any thing. Being is but a part of speech, a fixed symbol for a reality that is only and always shifting and becoming. There is no mountain, no man, no monkey, no midge—there is mountain*ing*, man*ing*, monkey*ing*, mid*ging* . . . at most the appearances of things, but in fact no *things,* only happenings.

OPPOSITE. Attributed to Mao Sung : *Monkey.* 12th c.

The world as we know it is a becoming, is ceaseless change. Change is the only unchanging fact. Science confirms it: *"There are no longer definite terms: a ceaseless becoming appears. Only change has a reality in itself, and it alone is found everywhere as a fundamental basis."* [30]

The findings of modern science may in this way seem to square with the statements of Lao Tsu, but in fact stop short of them. Ceaseless change can suggest chaos or a mechanical round, making of life a "tale told by an idiot . . . signifying nothing."

The Tao cannot be told, but its way can be seen as creative, not chaotic. There is no Creator, there is *Creativity*. In the light of this, the many fragments of the world fall into place to make a whole, and man finds his place wholly in it.

The way of Tao in the world is not as the rule of a Potentate or a Mechanic's strict ordering; it is as the way of a creative artist. For the artist manifestation is no burden but the way of creating, of being what he *is,* naturally. Nor does the density of material in any way make for degrees of creativity: what takes shape as a song is not more creative than what takes shape as the sculptor's granite. Each thing is unique and incomparable, created only in accordance with its own nature and kind. All forms of nature in being true to their own nature are true to the one Nature: "Tao is tao; tao is Tao."

Life weighs heavily on many of the religious; it is a burden that some seek to drop, becoming monks in distant monasteries, ascetics in the cold mountains. For others who remain among us, the burden is assumed and made acceptable by being borne for a noble cause, as the Christian with his cross. Rejected or accepted in this way, the world of becoming must nevertheless seem in some measure burdensome if reality is the *Being* of God.

If reality is *Creativity,* however, there is no burden in becoming. Creativity naturally assumes innumerable forms; it is its nature to do so. So the Tao brings the ten thousand things to light for no reason. Things are what they are for no reason. To call them good or bad describes only the mind that calls them so. The creative artist seeks only to show the reality of things, the life informing all forms—not Beauty but a pair of old boots, perhaps, shown in all the wonder of them when they are seen stripped of all associations, as for the first time on the first morning of the world. Awareness of the world *as it is* makes the world new.

OPPOSITE. Li Sung : *The Red Cliff.* 13th c.
BELOW. Shin Lin : *Landscape* (detail). 17th c.

As with beast and bird and flower, man finds freedom in being what he *is* by nature. Free men of this kind will seem strangers among us, so that we see them as supernatural beings. In old China, however, the sage was named the "Natural Man."

It is the nature of rivers to flow, birds to fly, a pen to write, a knife to cut. A blunt knife does not fulfill its function and so may be named "unnatural."[31]

So it is with man. He does not live according to his nature, that which is his alone. Nature in the eagle has come upon wings, in the tiger upon sharp claws and burning brightness, in the cricket upon its own kind of song. In man now, Nature has able hands and a new kind of awareness that can bear witness to all the wonder of things, can see and celebrate all the many appearances of the one Nature. "The maker of the song becomes its singer."[32]

Nature becomes conscious of itself in man at the moment when man becomes conscious of himself as Nature.[33] "Thus nature ceases to exist as a mere object. It becomes subject and object in one. It is nature that in the conscious, perceiving and creating man, the artist, who is himself nature, becomes aware of itself, experiences itself, insofar as it is perceptive. Thus the dichotomy of subject and object, of seeing and seen, is resolved: the two have become one."[34]

The end of evolution is not survival then, but consciousness of a kind that celebrates and so re-creates the world. In all other creatures, in all other things, nature's creative impulse is fulfilled, comes to an end in that thing. In man as creature it is the same, but man may be more than creaturely, he may be creative and so further Creativity, as the artist in seeing all things newly brings them to life. "I want to paint men and women with something of the eternal which the halo used to symbolize," said Van Gogh, and did as much for a yellow chair, a pair of boots.

To see with such eyes is not an objective exercise, not a scientific matter; it is participation. "In drawing a tree, the spread of its branches and leaves gives an awareness of my shoulders and arms and fingers and I feel its roots in my feet."[35]

This is not to say that all men must become artists if they are to come into their own; it is to say that all men *are* artists by nature. If only for the while that they paint or carve, artists are emptied of all that is old and told and done to death; they see as for the first time; they make new.

All men are by nature empty and so may see in this way. At any moment a man may awaken from the long sleep that his life must otherwise seem and find himself in that whole new world he has so long sought.

OPPOSITE. Wang Wen : *Two immortals and a three-legged toad.* 16th c.

ABOVE. Attributed to Ma Yuan : *The hermit fisherman.*
13th c.

Man's old dream of unity is then a fact to which he can waken. Waking, he brings it about. To *see* is to find the Peaceable Kingdom. Eden of the Four Rivers is the Great Emptiness of Lao Tsu, in us and all about us wherever we walk, whenever we walk with eyes unclouded by any division between ourselves and the world, when we are "truly skylike." "*The Natural Man is empty and so is everywhere.*"

Science now comes to confirm the reality of that dream: we are of the one Space that surrounds, enfolds, upholds, informs us, *is* us. We are all that is happening at every moment; inside and outside are but two aspects of a whole, as the lifting and lowering of the chest is one breathing.

Out of Space come all the ten thousand things, so that Space is all that we can imagine and mean by the word "God," if by that we mean all that is beyond all words, beyond all fixed, still images; no Creator but Creativity. God and the world, as the world and oneself,

are one happening here and now and always in all ways. "*Tao is in an ant, in a blade of grass, in a roof tile, in dung,*" said Chuang Tsu. "*Don't try to find it, for you'll not find it apart from the ten thousand things.*"

Insofar as we are at all, we are our appearances. Appearances apart, we are no thing; we are Emptiness. Emptiness is the unmanifest aspect of things, as things are the manifest aspect of Emptiness. Those who turn from the appearances of things to find Reality must wander as blindly as those who, seeking only appearances, lose sight of Reality. However Reality appears, it is here, now, and we are It.

The world that we are is not to be known by us, for to know it would be to stand apart from it. Science now knows that it cannot know. Knowledge is only "knowledge of structural form and not knowledge of content. All through the physical world runs that unknown content, which must surely be the stuff of our consciousness."[36]

That content is not only unknown, it is unknowable. But in the light of it, all things are known. The artist Hokusai, at the end of a long life, joyously exclaimed: "At last I do not know how to draw!" At any moment of one's life one may come upon the end of oneself and no longer know how to live, as the gray seal in the blue wide bay does not know how to swim, and the black shag dives deep without knowing how, and the white gull, ignorant of how to fly, does not try, nor worry whence and where and to what end it lives and flies and dies.

All that men strain and strive to become is at best as unnecessary as "painting red roses red." At worst it is unnatural. Striving to be "spiritual" by whatever means is "putting legs on a snake." One cannot strive to be natural, for striving is unnatural. To see this is to cease to strive. "*Cease striving and there will be transformation.*" Empty of every wish to be other than we are, we are already other than we were. All that the religions have reached after is already given as grace, if we will have the grace to see it.

Boundless as the sky . . .
But here it is, right here, profound and clear.
Seek it, and you will not see it.[37]

There is nothing to be done but to see that there is nothing to be done, and no one to do it. To see this is Emptiness. All that the religious do to be rid of self is like *"shouting at an echo to stop."* When the way is as water falling, the images of religion that show a man bearing the load of his life and bravely toiling up a steep mountainside to Truth would seem ridiculous if they were not tragic. *"Tao in the world is like a river flowing home to the sea,"* said Lao Tsu. *"Gravity is the root of grace."*

BELOW. Ma Yuan : *The fir branch.* 12th–13th c.

In search of meaning, men in the West have looked out and about themselves, have lifted their eyes off the earth to God in his heaven, or they have wandered in the many winding paths of philosophy or have looked to logic, or to science for the secret of the life of things. Some ways of the East have gone to other extremes: wise Indians have shut their eyes on the turning, temporal world to find what is only Absolute and Eternal.

The old Chinese preferred to fish. And not merely to catch fish, for that can make of the rare moment only a means to an end. Each moment is whole, each activity its own end. One does not fish to catch fish—that may or may not follow. Content with what may or may not be, the fisherman has all he could ever want or need. Contentment is all. For fishing of this kind, even no hook is needed; at most a piece of string perhaps, if one can care to call it "fishing." Such a fisherman exists without aid of hook or belief or single thought in the full wonder of Emptiness. In Emptiness he sits as in a Sung painting, at ease in all the immensity of Space without any visible means of support, sits and smiles and lets the line out. The sun shines, or it does not shine. The one breeze bends the reeds by the shore and sways his beard. Mountains rise around and are reflected in the water. A bird flies over with a cry that increases silence. His heart is still as his mind is, reflecting all. Reflecting all, he is himself whole.

To fish in this way is to play. To play is to live wholly and abundantly. "To play means to devote oneself so completely to the psychic process that one becomes its body: the psychic finds its fulfillment in the physical, and becomes form."[38] "In the form and function of play, man's consciousness that he is embedded in a sacred order of things finds its first, highest and holiest expression."[39]

Since there is no purpose in it, it is Emptiness that makes possible all forms of play. All forms *are* play. In Emptiness there is space for anything and everything: anything may come about, anything may be. Nothing has special meaning. In a world where nothing has special meaning, all is equally meaningful. The Natural Man is not more of a Buddha when he brings miracles about or less of a Christ when he goes behind a bush to obey, as the saying goes, "the call of Nature." In all he does he obeys the call of Nature.

ABOVE AND BELOW. Ku Yuan : parts of a long scroll, *The poetry competition*. 19th c.

There can be no serious answers to questions about the meaning of life, for to ask about life is to stand back from life and pretend one is not it. Questions at best are a form of play, and may be enjoyed as such. They are best answered by players, by the artists and poets among us:

What is Life?
The mountain pears are tiny but ripe.
What is Man?
A Tartar flute plays by the city gate.
What is Death?
A single wild goose climbs into the void.[40]

There are no right answers, only light ones, given and taken lightly by those who know that they play. The "Enlightened" man is not other than the fool. What makes a man enlightened is the realization that he is as a fool. *"My mind is that of a fool,"* said Lao Tsu. *"How empty it is!"*

Set beside the solemn scriptures of the world, the words of Lao Tsu and of Chuang Tsu must seem to lack seriousness. This is the truth of them. Emptiness takes nothing seriously, raises no one thing up over another. Worshipping nothing, it celebrates all.

Worship looks beyond things to some Absolute for which the things of the world may at best be said to stand, to symbolize. Emptiness looks nowhere; it sees what is to be seen, as it is, here and now. Being clear and uncolored by thoughts about and about things, it sees things clearly in all their true colors and many kinds. In Emptiness, all things that may at most have seemed "instinct with life and light," come to light and actual life.

"We are the mind, ultimately, of Space." Being by nature skylike, transparent and clear,

we are able to shed light on all the ten thousand things, to make them new. Moreover, simply to "consider the lilies" is a creative act that can renew ourselves.

The Way was told by Jesus wandering in Galilee; it was told by Lao Tsu among the high mountains of China, and by Thoreau wandering by Walden Pond: "If for a moment we make way with our petty selves, wish no ill to anyone, apprehend no ill, cease to be but as a crystal which reflects a ray—what shall we not reflect! What a universe will appear crystallized and radiant around us!"

It was told on the bathtub of the Emperor T'ang, in letters of gold it was told:

新日日新

AS THE SUN MAKES IT NEW   DAY BY DAY MAKE IT NEW   AND AGAIN MAKE IT NEW

41

OPPOSITE. Liang K'ai : *Putai.* 13th c. Though himself poor and unassuming, he carries a great bottomless bag with treasures for one and all. "He is innocence itself, a veritable image of egolessness, of freedom and humour."—D. T. Suzuki.

REFERENCES

1. GEORGE ROWLEY : *Principles of Chinese Painting*
2. All italicized quotations of this kind are from translations of Taoist texts attributed to Lao Tsu and Chuang Tsu.
3. SIMONE WEIL : *Gravity and Grace*
4. ALDOUS HUXLEY : *Those Barren Leaves*
5. SAMUEL BECKETT quoted in "The Reality of Nothing" by Roy Finch. *The Lugano Review*, 1965
6. RAINER MARIA RILKE : *Duino Elegies*, translated by J. B. Leishman and Stephen Spender
7. DEMETRIOS CAPETANAKIS in *Demetrios Capetanakis*, edited by John Lehman
8. A. S. EDDINGTON : *The Nature of the Physical World*
9. JAMES JEANS : *The Mysterious Universe*
10. LINCOLN BARNETT : *The Universe and Dr. Einstein*
11. BERTRAND RUSSELL quoted in *The Roots of Coincidence* by ARTHUR KOESTLER
12. JOHN PFEIFFER : *The Changing Universe*
13. A. S. EDDINGTON : *The Nature of the Physical World*
14. PIERRE ROUSSEAU quoted in *Living Zen* by ROBERT LINSSEN
15. A. S. EDDINGTON : *The Nature of the Physical World*
16. ARTHUR KOESTLER : *The Roots of Coincidence*
17. SHAKESPEARE : *Cymbeline*
18. HAROLD SPENCER-JONES in broadcast talk reported in *The Listener*, London, July 1952
19. A. S. EDDINGTON : *The Nature of the Physical World*
20. G. SPENCER BROWN : *Laws of Form*
21. DENIS SAURAT : *The End of Fear*
22. ARTHUR WALEY : *Zen Buddhism and Its Relation to Art*
23. MICHAEL SULLIVAN : *The Birth of Landscape Painting in China*
24. Eighth-century Chinese verse quoted in *Creativity and Taoism* by CHANG CHUNG-YUAN
25. FRED HOYLE : *Frontiers of Astronomy*
26. ABBOT OBORA quoted in *The Tiger's Cave* by TREVOR LEGGETT
27. D. H. LAWRENCE : *Pansies*
28. Ch'anist saying quoted in *Creativity and Taoism* by CHANG CHUNG-YUAN
29. TUNG YU
30. EDOUARD LE ROY quoted in *Living Zen* by ROBERT LINSSEN
31. See E. A. WODEHOUSE : "Man, Nature, Reality in the Teachings of Krishnamurti," *Star Bulletin*, 1931
32. Ibid.
33. See MAX SCHELER : *Man's Place in Nature*
34. M. C. CAMMERLOHER : "The Position of Art in the Psychology of Our Time," *Eranos Yearbook* 4
35. MARION MILNER : *On Not Being Able to Paint*
36. A. S. EDDINGTON : *The Nature of the Physical World*
37. YUNGCHIA TASHIH : *Chengtaoke*
38. M. C. CAMMERLOHER : "The Position of Art in the Psychology of Our Time," *Eranos Yearbook* 4
39. JOHAN HUIZINGA : *Homo Ludens*
40. The three italicized lines are from a poem by TU FU translated by Kenneth Rexroth.
41. Translation by Ezra Pound

The Way of Things

ABOVE. Tomikichiro Tokuriki : Illustration from a series
of *Ten Bulls*. 20th c.

3 The Way of Things

I have never practiced the swami's technique for "heightening consciousness" and I doubt that I ever shall. For one thing, I am not sure that I want to be so exclusively aware of either myself or the All in the colorless essence of either. To put it in a dignified way, I prefer to live under the dome of many-colored glass and to rest content with the general conviction that the white radiance of eternity has something to do with it. To put it more familiarly, what I am after is less to meet God face to face than really to take in a beetle, a frog, or a mountain when I meet one.

JOSEPH WOOD KRUTCH

I'm all for the cosmos. I'll go, too—but with a rose in my hand.

Young Russian girl, 1965

A MAN TOOK A FLOWER ONCE AND without a word held it up before the men seated in a circle about him. Each man in his turn looked at the flower, and then explained its meaning, its significance, all that it symbolized. The last man, however, *seeing* the flower, said nothing, only smiled. The man in the center then also smiled and, without a word, handed him the flower.

The origins of Zen are said to lie in this. That the man in the center happened to be the Buddha does not matter. Zen is what happens when any man anywhere at any time *sees*.

Zen has no history as happiness has no history. Zen is what shows when we leave aside all concepts, all the appurtenances of philosophy and religion, to see what is before us—a Buddha, a flower, a beggar, a fly in the eye of a cow. The smile that naturally follows is one of the fruits of Zen.

Zen is simply seeing simply. It is not a way *to* see, not a system, not a discipline, not a spiritual method. To see any one thing is to see all, for *seeing is all*. "I" do not see; seeing is what I AM before Abraham was, and Gautama and Jesus; it is what all things, all beings *are*—whether they see it or not.

Zen is said to be seeing into one's own Nature, and so into the nature of all things. Seeing any one thing, one loses oneself to find oneself *as* all things. Awake in this way, one is not only at home in the Universe, one is it. Small wonder there is smiling.

The West today hears overmuch talk of Zen. Here is yet more. One can only talk of Zen. Zen cannot be told. But it is not therefore a matter of saying nothing. If sages are for the most part silent, the sleeping and the dead are wholly so, and not necessarily the wiser for it. The man of Zen was not silent when he was asked: What is Zen? He answered emphatically, unequivocally, appositely: "Have a cup of tea."

To the endless questions of others asking the nature of Zen, innumerable answers have been given: *The cypress tree in the courtyard. A dumpling. Plum blossom. Dried dung. The head of a dead cat.* Clearly any answer will do:

OPPOSITE. Chu Ta : *Beetle on a banana leaf.* 17th c.

81

When the question is sand in a bowl of boiled rice
The answer is a stick in soft mud.

But it must be *any* answer, not one that is in any way premeditated or intended to put an end to the question. Any answer, seen for what it is, puts an end to the questioner.

Any answer will not, however, come from any man, but only from one who when asked: What is Zen? What is God? Man? Nature? Life? Death? sees clearly that "when the white heron stands in the snow, it has a different color."

The religions of the world tend to turn from the sight and smell and touch and taste and sound of the things of the world. At most they seek meaning in things, so to find "tongues in trees, books in running brooks, sermons in stones and good in everything." One finds what one seeks, alas, and only that. One finds tongues, books, sermons, and good, but the trees, the brooks, the stones are missed, the bad is overlooked, the ten thousand things are lost. It is to these that Zen points.

The religions of the world point out that things are but transitory; all the brightness of the rose is for a while only; the mayfly comes in the morning and in the evening is dead, is gone. God does not come and go, therefore seek God only. Zen, however, looks to what is momentary and only mortal—the drop of a lark from the sky, the smell of the laurel, a stranger's look, a cry on the wind, the very wind.

The religions of the world in their various ways turn then from what is transitory and

material to seek Eternal Spirit, turn from the shadows of the many things to find the One Light of the world. Nicholas of Cusa has, however, pointed out that "the word for God (Deus) comes from *theoro*, meaning *I see*. For God in our world is like vision in the world of color. Color is not perceived except by vision, and in order that the center of sight may attain freely to every color, is itself without color. In the realm of color, vision is not to be found. Hence in relation to the realm of color, vision is more properly called *nothing* than something."

Light is not a thing and so may not be sought. It is nothing and so may not be found anywhere but everywhere. To see anything wholly is to find the light that is on all things, is in them, *is* them. "The tendency of modern physics," said James Jeans, "is to reduce the whole Universe to waves, and nothing but waves. These waves are of two kinds: captive waves which we call matter, and free waves which we call light. These concepts reduce the whole Universe to a world of potential or real light."[1]

A man of Zen was visited by a monk who said that he had come from the Monastery of Spiritual Light. "In the daytime, we have sunlight," said the man of Zen. "In the evening, we have lamplight. What is Spiritual Light?" The monk could not answer, so that the man of Zen spoke for him: "Sunlight, lamplight."

BELOW. Ashikaga Kano School : *Landscape, bird, flowers, trees, and waves* (detail). 15th–16th c.

The man of vision, this man of Zen, is more properly called *Nobody* than somebody. "Look at empty space. It is in emptiness that light is born."[2] The man of Zen, being "wholly empty, and nothing holy," lives without preference or judgment, as the sun itself in a world where all things may be seen to play their necessary parts. To find the world whole in this way is to have ceased seeking any one part of it. Without seeking, there is no seeker; with no one standing in the way, the light is freely allowed, all the ten thousand things are revealed. The secret, said Grock the clown, lies in seeing the world "every day of one's life as though for the very first time. The rest comes automatically. . . . I have only to walk across a marketplace for all the apples to begin to jump about in their baskets . . . old, discarded pianos thrum audibly when I enter the room they stand in . . . I have only to appear in their midst for the ladies of the neighbourhood to increase the population."[3]

The mind of man logically insists that something cannot come from nothing. The philosopher Martin Heidegger has asked: "Why is there something and not nothing?" There is something *because* there is Nothing. Or, as a man of Zen would say: "Have a cup of tea."

The nature of all things is Void, says Zen. Science now assures us of it: "When the environment of space and time and matter, of light and color and concrete things is probed deeply by every device of physical science, at the bottom we reach symbols. Its substance has melted into shadow."[4]

This is a half-truth. The other half is the substance that "shadow" assumes. Space shows in time as all the ten thousand things. *Void is form; form is Void.* Uniquely among the "spiritual" ways of the world, Zen has out of an empty sleeve brought forth a plenty of material things, and not things made only in the service of religion, but things in themselves: teapots and rock gardens, bamboo back-scratchers, iron tools, handicrafts of all kinds, and works of art that can seem more as works of nature, as indeed they are, since they come from the hands and heart and minds-at-large of natural men.

While the roots of Zen lie in the Void, its flowering shows when a man sees the world as for the first time with the eyes of his Original Face. It happens out of time. In time, however, Zen may also bear fruit. It happened in China twelve centuries ago. A few men there outgrew their infancy and knew nothing of Zen; as every man they thought that "mountains were mountains, rivers were rivers, trees were trees." The world seemed full of a number of things; as every man they sleepwalked in that world, fetched water, chopped wood.

In time, however, they came to know something of Zen and so awakened from that dream of their every day to see that "mountains were no longer mountains, rivers were not rivers anymore, trees were not trees"; they seemed as nothing, they seemed void.

Looking on, however, they came to see that the world was indeed Void, themselves the same. Knowing Zen thoroughly now, they knew the Void as flying birds know air, as swimming fish know water. Void of all ideas, undeceived by dreams, no longer crippled by concepts, they saw the world for what it *is:* "mountains were mountains, rivers were rivers, trees were trees." And knowing now the Reality of the world, they went in wonder about the business of their every day:

> *How wondrously supernatural,*
> *and how miraculous this:*
> *I fetch water! I chop wood!*[5]

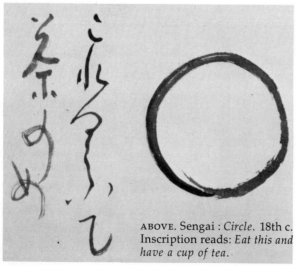

ABOVE. Sengai : *Circle.* 18th c. Inscription reads: *Eat this and have a cup of tea.*

OPPOSITE. Kang Hui-an : *Sage in meditation.* 15th c.

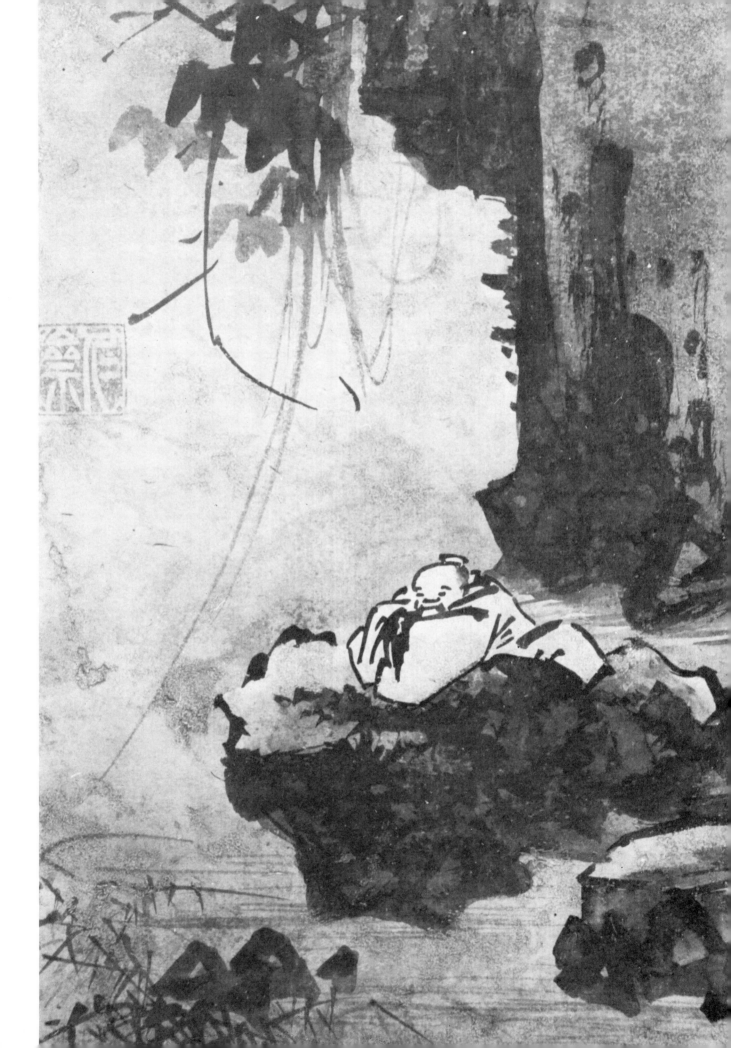

Some men, moved by the same wonder, took up brushes and put upon paper and silk images that gave some hint of their happiness to find Reality all as real as a frog beneath a banana leaf, a lone monkey in the rain. The Void proved to be the plenitude of things. The appearance of things was their Reality. "There is another world," said the poet Paul Eluard, "but it is in this one." More can be said: There is another world—*it is this one.*

"The Western spirit accepts the reality of the material world; the Western man sees in it something to be used, forces to be harnessed, pleasures to be enjoyed. The art of the West is full of a vivid sense of the glory of the visible world, still more of the beauty of human being and human activity. But beyond the beauty of shining streams and green meadows and showy trees and blue hills lies something from which it recoils: Space, the all-enveloping infinite, unexplored Space. . . . Here is nothing it can use or deal with."[6]

The spirit of Zen knows the Reality of the material world, and so does not dream to use it, only to reveal it. The space in a Zen painting is a natural way to do it, for space mirrors that Void which is all that the mind can conceive as Reality.

In these "one-corner" paintings, three parts are given to space. This is not to give more importance to the Void than to the lone crow in the one corner; the Void does not overwhelm the crow, on the contrary, it draws attention to it: there is nothing else! The crow for its part reveals the Void, makes clear the space that surrounds it. But Void and crow are not two things as these words imply, nor are they one thing as the mind may next suggest. "When all things are reduced to the One, what is the One reduced to?"

> *When they are not two things,*
> *they are not one thing,*
> *and the wind*
> *in the ink picture*
> *is cool indeed.*[7]

OPPOSITE. Nonomura Sotatsu : *The Zen priest Choka*.
17th c.

RIGHT. Mu Ch'i : *Shrike on a bare pine branch*.
13th c.

ABOVE. Fugai : *Tanka burning the Buddha.* 19th c.

ABOVE. Liang K'ai : *Ch'an priest.* 13th c.

The first essential of painting, said Kuo Jo-shu, is "to show the Cosmic Spirit in its rhythmical activity. Other essentials may be acquired by study, but that Spirit is an inborn quality and no amount of skill can reveal it, nor will the lapse of years make one its owner. If it is found at all, it is found in the silent spaces of the painter's being. He comes upon it without knowing how, when, or where." The Spirit, as the wind, bloweth where it listeth.

This emphasis on Spirit determined the course of Zen painting, what was done and how it was done. There were no enthroned Buddhas painted or heavenly beings, but crazy men or fellow monks burning statues of a Buddha to warm their backsides, or tearing up the scriptures. "The scriptures are useful to wipe dirt from the skin," it was said. Zen paintings showed it. The forms of religion were mocked lest the Spirit be confused with them and men be bound by them. Men pass from the bondage of "material" things to a bondage of "spiritual" things. Held by this world, we are within a leaden cage; held by that world we are in a golden cage. A cage is a cage. So Zen insists: "If you utter the word *Buddha,* wash out your mouth!"

Iconoclastic in content, some Zen paintings

can seem as careless of form; it looks as if the ink was flung down upon the paper. So it was. A painter, Cheng Jung, noted for the simplicity of his life and the competence with which he fulfilled his duties as a magistrate (facts that should not be overlooked), was also known for his love of wine and for paintings done under the influence of high spirits of one sort or another. He threw down a splash of ink to make clouds, spat out water to make mists, uttered a great shout, and seized his hat for a brush. Other painters took up fistfuls of straw. Wang Hei plunged his head in a bucket of ink, and flopped it on the silk—as if by magic, mountains rose up, rivers flowed, trees swayed in the wind.

There are also paintings in ink upon pieces of thin absorbent paper that allow no pause for thought, no erasure. To paint a bird one must partake of its nature. The bird does not pause in flight to ponder the rightness or wrongness of the tilt of its wings; it flies on, it flies on. The artist who stops to wonder how, finds no bird on the paper, only a blot. This, says Zen, is not only a way of painting, it is the art of life, the way of living, the way of a bird, of life as it flies. To the question: What is Zen? the answer was given: Walk on!

Zen paintings can seem to have come into being as naturally as the willows they depict, as easily as the smile that comes to the face of one who sees them. They are not of nature so much as *by* nature; they are not willed works of art. As the sun shines and the pine branch casts a shadow, the artist is empty of all intention. He is Void. The rest follows:

See, the paper-shutter is clean of every speck of dust:
How perfect is the shadow of the pine-trees![8]

Empty as the paper before him, void of all preferences for or against, the Zen painter is free to delight in all things. Free of any fixed point of view, the painter moves freely over the landscape, among mountains, rivers, trees; he is free of that obsession with perspective that refers all things back to the Western painter standing still in one place. There is no place even for the viewer to stand and look at a Zen painting; he must enter and wander there. "Awaken the mind without fixing it anywhere." In Zen paintings there is no painter to cast his shadow over the world; each thing stands revealed in the Clear Light of the Void. "The material thing before you, that is IT," said Huang Po.

But words are not things; immaterial and fragmentary as the mind they come from, they break, scatter, and make insubstantial the very things they mean to tell of. The word "owl" is without feathers to fly, it does not perch or hoot in the night, it does not swoop; the word "mouse" does not *scream*.

If words do not live, move, and have being, how shall they tell of the living being of any thing? How shall they tell of the lively Being of all things? They cannot, but taken for what they are—fragments—they can nevertheless be shown as fragments of the Whole, as the first faint curve of the new moon points to the full round and radiant harvest moon.

In such a way, a man of Zen in the guise of a poet takes only seventeen syllables to make a *haiku* and brings the whole world about. "A *haiku* is not a poem, it is not literature; it is a hand beckoning, a door half-opened, a mirror wiped clean. It is a way of returning to nature, to our moon nature, our cherry blossom nature, our falling leaf nature, in short to our Buddha nature. It is a way in which the cold winter rain, the swallows of evening, even the very day in its hotness, and the length of the night become truly alive, share in our humanity, speak their own silent, expressive language."[9]

90

The appreciation of a *haiku* can seem to involve all the tears one has shed and the laughter, all war and peace, the living and the dying of one's days, nightmare and silent night, holy night, but *haiku* are nothing if they do not waken. One can bring all the wisdom of all one's years to the moment of a *haiku* and yet miss the point.

The poet Basho once told of a time and a place:

> *An old pond.*
> *A frog jumps in.*
> *Plop!*

These few words have been the cause of many. Long and weighty explanations have been given. One can think on these few things and find in them all manner of things. But busied with such solemn considerations, one misses the point: the poet's pointing to the old pond, the frog . . . one misses the *plop!*

The splash occurs in time and out of time. Eternity for the man of Zen is an immediate and present fact as the evidence of his eyes is for any man who sees at all. Clearly, "Eternity is in love with the productions of time," so that the man of Zen is as a man in love; he is as a fool who loves what must be lost, and so for the little while that he lives, he lives eternally. Bent by the years so that he knows he must soon die, he bends further to plant acorns and apple seeds. When the bombs rain down, he is reminded to go out and water his garden.

OPPOSITE LEFT. Zeshin : *Rat.* 19th c.
OPPOSITE RIGHT. Zeshin : *Monkey and rainbow.* 19th c.
BELOW. Hiroshige School : *Travelers in a landscape.* 19th c.

The poetry of Zen lies in the holy poverty of things; the wonder lies in their transitoriness, their fragility, their ordinariness, their nothingness. A Japanese has said: "One must understand the Ah! of things."

Such understanding does not come easily to us in the West. We are reared in operatic attitudes, instructed in a gospel of use, so that if things are not in some way "extraordinary," they are only "ordinary." But Zen, with its roots in the Void, flowers in an extraordinary attention given to ordinary things, bears fruit in common acts uncommonly done.

This is perhaps most apparent in the drinking of tea, an act for most of us accompanied by the clatter of cups and interminable chatter. One enters a Japanese tearoom as we would think to enter a chapel. The approach is through a tranquil garden and one enters by way of so small a door that one must go on one's knees and lower one's head. The room, of rough woodwork and plain walls, is about ten feet square and bare of all but a single flower in a vase, or a painting that is in itself many parts space. These few things emphasize the emptiness, as the emptiness draws attention to the few things. The tearoom is named "The Abode of Vacancy." One sits very still on the floor to sip a bitter brew from a small, crudely shaped bowl. It is hard to understand how anything so spare and bare as the Japanese tea ceremony could influence a whole culture as it did.

There are no words to tell of Zen, but there are a few words that can in some way suggest the wonder of things, the Ah! of things. *Wabi* is one word. It is not to be translated but words among us such as simple, serene, unpretentious, stripped and still, can move us a little way toward the meaning of *wabi*. There is also a verse by a man of Tea which says:

> *If you have one pot*
> *and you make your tea with it,*
> *that will do quite well.*
> *How much a man lacks*
> *who must have many things.*

Henry David Thoreau said as much: "A man is rich in proportion to the number of things he can afford to let alone." We have called wealth of this kind "holy poverty." *Wabi* is of this kind, but there is also in it a wistfulness born of the clear understanding that all things lovely are subject to loss and oblivion; the beauty of things involves heartbreak. This is not a matter to be bemoaned: "the poetry is in the pity."

The mortality of things makes for the life of them. Artificial flowers do not die and so are deathly indeed. Joy and sadness are interwined in the Ah! of things.

Another word associated with tea drinking is *sabi;* it implies "mellowed by use," and so runs counter to all that is slick and shining. Time, says a Japanese proverb, is unkind to man, but kind to things. The age of things adds to their beauty. The presence of old things makes for quiet in us. *Sabi* is in unpainted wood, in woven straw, in bark and mossy stones; it can even mean rusty and so rejected, and so it can also mean lonely. Time carries all away; the works of man pass with him, but the love of old things can bring a realization that it is also given to man to face gracefully his fate as a creature of time haunted by eternity. Those who cannot grow old with grace are without *sabi.*

OPPOSITE LEFT. Entrance to tea garden, Katsura Palace, Kyoto.
OPPOSITE RIGHT. Entrance to tea room, Koto-in, Kyoto.
ABOVE. Interior of Kokyuan tea house, Kyoto.

Things that have both *wabi* and *sabi* may be described by a third word, *shibui,* meaning astringent, a little sour, or as a very dry wine. But it can be applied to anything and everything: to cooking and to clothes as to the way one behaves. What is *shibui* is simple, austere, plain, with an inner presence not to be explained by its outward form. A *shibui* thing will appear born rather than made; it is earthy and commonplace; it implies a love of material, of things as they are, as they have come from nature.

It is in the things that we look upon every day that we can sense what cannot be seen: THIS that is not born and does not die and *is*, now and always. In the pity and the stark poetry of things lies the clearest hint of THIS— in a cracked cup, in an old log destined for the fire. All things tell of THIS. By way of what is shown, what cannot be shown is felt as a living presence. There is no God. If there were a God he would be but one Thing among the many things; at best he would be but one Being among the many beings. It is the absence of God that makes his presence felt. So Basho told it:

> *Along the road*
> *Goes no one*
> *This autumn eve . . .*

Poems of this kind are written in the reader. The poet sees and points, leads us a little way, and leaves us to see for ourselves. Asked to preach a sermon on the Meaning of Existence, a man of Zen took one step forward and opened wide his arms.

ABOVE. Sand garden, Ryoanji temple, Kyoto.

LEFT. Path in grounds of moss temple, Kokedera, Kyoto.

94

We may stand in the same way on the veranda of the Zen Buddhist temple of Ryoanji to see its garden: a great rectangle of raked sand with a few rocks arising from it. The garden has been likened to "unaccompanied Bach."[10] It has been described as "a direct journey into the void from which all is born, an absurd chaste embrace of the mathematics of the heavenly spheres."[11]

As with Zen paintings, as with Zen poems, there have been explanations: the fifteen carefully chosen rocks are said to be figures from the Buddhist pantheon, or they are Buddhist Principles; their careful arrangement into five groups is a Parable. The expanse of sand is the same Void that was shown in the space of the paintings, in the silence of the poet's old pond. But to speak of these things in this way is to deny them; to tell of the Void in this way is to make an abstraction of it, not "a fact of experience as much as the straightness of a bamboo and the redness of a flower."[12]

Sand is sand. Rock is rock. "A rose is a rose is a rose." What more shall one ask them to be?

There are those who stand in awe of art but not of nature, who will be still and breathless before a stretch of raked sand but walk, if they should ever do so, upon a seaside beach unseeingly. The worth of art is that it may shock us into *seeing*—into seeing anything and everything, not art alone.*

*Art is a concrete and personal and rather childish thing after all—no matter what people do to graft it into science and make it sociological and psychological; it is no good at all unless it is let alone to be itself—a game of make-believe, or re-production, very exciting and delightful to people who have an ear for it or an eye for it. Art is too terribly human to be very "great" perhaps. Some very big artists have outgrown art, the men were bigger than the game. Tolstoi did, and Leonardo did. Shakespeare died at fifty-two, but there is an awful veiled threat in *The Tempest,* that he too felt he had outgrown his toys, was about to put them away and free that spirit of Comedy and Lyrical Poetry and all the rest he held captive—quit play-making and verse-making forever and turn his attention—to what, he did not hint, but it was probably merely to enjoy with all his senses that Warwickshire country which he loved to weakness—with a warm physical appetite. WILLA CATHER: *Light on Adobe Walls.*

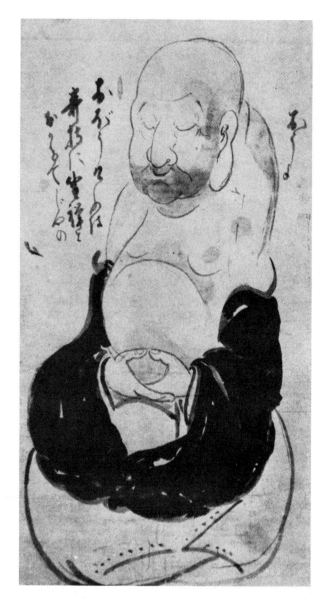

ABOVE. Hakuin : *Self-portrait in zazen* (sitting-meditation). 18th c. Inscription reads:
> "Hey, bonze!
> Wonder of wonders:
> You're doing zazen today."
> "Sure!"

ABOVE RIGHT. Monks awaiting interview with Zen master.

RIGHT. Sengai : *The meditating frog.* 18th c. Inscription reads: *If a man becomes a Buddha by practising zazen . . .*
[Frog though I am, I'd have been a Buddha long ago.]

Men of Zen have warned of "too much Zen," even of the "stink of Zen." It may well hang about a stretch of sand that must be maintained by monks against the wind, swept of fallen leaves and all signs of insurgent, untidy life, combed into strict predetermined patterns with rakes of a special design. It hovers surely above the shaven heads of monks rigidly squatting in ordered ranks to sweat after *satori*. The sea knows nothing of Zen Buddhism and the wind blows where it will over the beach, making patterns that are always new and for the first and only time, and only for a time, until the careless sea sweeps clean and bare again, and again leaves a new stretch for a new beginning, for a new and another wind to play upon for a while. Arrested by religion, Zen begins to stink as river water in a bowl, as wind in a box.

Life is lost in all forms that last. In understanding of this, Zen itself seeks to shatter all forms, to undo divinity: "If you meet the Buddha on the road—kill him!" But this is only the other side of subservience and deep bowing. Beyond the worship of the Buddha's form, and of the murder of the Buddha in the cause of formlessness, lies Informality: If you should by chance meet the Buddha, smile and shake his hand; walk with him then over the hills to the sanctum of a pub—a Pilgrim's Inn, perhaps, a *Maison Dieu*, as such places were once called; if he declines to enter, sit with him in the sun on a bench outside and talk of the ten thousand things, or do not talk but simply raise your glass of wine to his of lemon juice—every man to his own thing and the sun on us all: Buddha and Adam and Eve and all Eden here for the seeing. This may seem to be taking the Buddha lightly. How else shall one take a man of Light?

Zen at its best has brought about miracles of simplicity, giving a strong and lively grace to the everyday forms of pots and pans and men and women of Zen. At its worst, Zen has become only formal, giving such worship to outward form that the life within is lost; the strong grace of the swaying willow gives way to the rigidity of the sword. It is the story of all the religions of the world.

RIGHT. Shubun : *Kanzan and Jittoku;* Zen poet-recluses. 15th c.

We may, however, be saved from the "stink of Zen" by the smile of Zen. In Zen, says Nancy Wilson Ross, laughter is not merely permitted, it is insisted upon. "It is possible to read the Bible without a smile, and the Koran without a chuckle. No one has died of laughing while reading the Buddhist sutras. But Zen writing abounds in anecdotes that stimulate the diaphragm. Enlightenment is frequently accompanied by laughter of a transcendental kind which may further be described as a laughter of surprised approval. . . . Laughter is a state of being here and also everywhere, an infinite and timeless explosion of all oppression of our person and that of others, even of God, who is indeed laughed away."[13]

The laughter of Zen is as a gust of wind that lifts the royal robes to reveal the ankles of Everyman, the common feet of clay. This is not the schoolboy's wish to throw snowballs at top hats, to drop banana skins before bishops; not that alone. Zen does not condemn clay—on the contrary; it reveres all that is held commonplace, all everyday material things. Zen smiles when the fine pot tries to hide its earthly origin; it laughs at all pomposity.

"Seen from Spirit, nothing is heavy; it takes all things lightly. . . . Thus in the first place, spiritual man must impress man of earth as wanting in seriousness."[14]

But if a man of Zen can be called "spiritual," he is all the while most certainly a "man of earth," and his smiling is not of a shallow or superior wit, but compounded of all earthly experience, all the laughter and the tears of things. The world is so full of a number of things—common colds and uncommon deaths, broken hearts, uprisings and bloody revolutions—we should all be as miserable as presidents. The man of Zen, however, does not suffer these things for he knows no separation from them. Suffering is the last guise and refuge of the self. I suffer, therefore I exist. A man will give up everything except the suffering he gains by giving up everything. Not to suffer can seem not to exist; it is to have no being apart from the pity and the glory of things; it is to hammer eagerly with the sharp beak of the thrush while knowing the snail's agony in the broken shell; it is to struggle desperately with the worm, then to die and be digested and give thanks in the satisfied robin.

The man of Zen neither laughs at the world nor weeps over it; he *is* the world in all its joy and in its weeping; he is a man of sorrows with the morning stars shouting for joy. Every sorrow puts another song into his mouth, a sad song but a song, nevertheless. Under the full burden of grief, he walks lightly, for he has grown careless of comfort, of himself and so of his own salvation. How could he wish to be saved from a world that he is? Shall the eye start from the head in order to be saved from it, to find enlightenment for itself? Shall the hand reach out to be free? the little finger seek its own liberation? The man of Zen does not live in the world, he *is* it. When pain shows in the world, pain is what he knows; wherever joy is, that joy is his, for a while. For a while only. Holding to nothing, he wanders on.

Whether sad for a while or for a while joyful, he walks in wonder always, for to know that one is nothing makes everything wonderful: wonderful to have been born, to have put in an appearance at all! And with this unexpected appearance, the sun also shows, and rain, and health and sickness, black nights and, by dawn light, singing birds; here are bread and wine, broken men and flowing blood, here the heart beats faster for sight of the sparrow hawk; here it breaks over the sparrow's fall.

God knows, the gift of life is one that no man of Zen can see himself deserving. It is not in the number of things that we are given, but in our gratitude for whatever is given. So it was once said among us: "To them that hath shall be given." Zen knows, those who have nothing but gratitude have all things. "What injustice—the learned complain—that a drunkard, a laughing girl or drowsy old man may, by grace, come closer to the mystery than all those philosophers who climb the ladder rung by rung and would, if they were made immortal, still be climbing to the end of time."[15]

OPPOSITE. Sengai : *Buddha-possessed.* 18th c. Inscription reads: *Throughout the night, I have been annoyed by the thoughts of nirvana and samsara: apparently I had been made captive of Buddha.* "In Zen we speak of being over-possessed by goodness or holiness. Every kind of obsession is considered undesirable. . . . Sengai depicts himself as Hotei (Putai) awaking from a long and exhausting nightmare such as is described above."
—D. T. Suzuki.

BELOW. Shohaku : *Sage in a boat.* 18th c.

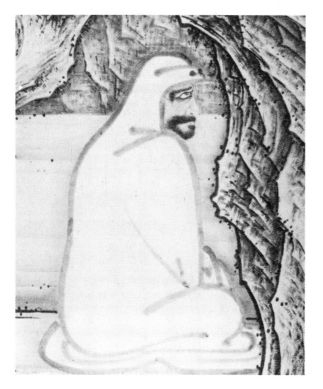

ABOVE LEFT. Sesshu : *Bodhidharma* (Daruma). Detail from *Hui-k'o offering his arm to Bodhidharma*. 15th c.
ABOVE RIGHT. Bodhidharma (Daruma) as a doll. 20th c.

There's no justice in a sun that so lacks discrimination it can shine on a black street-corner whore and make her sing soft and sing low, while pale monks on Mount Athos who have so magnificently renounced all women must miserably kneel in their cells; it is not fair that tramps and fools should feel free to roam the bright world while Zen novitiates must sit daylong in the dark to seek freedom and enlightenment; nor that lunatics, lovers, and wayward poets should go naked under the sun as no good Pope is permitted.

Bodhidharma, the twenty-eighth Patriarch in direct succession to the Buddha himself, strode sternly over the high Himalayas to bring to China the knowledge of the True Law. Known in Japan as Daruma and revered by Zen Buddhists, he is by plain folk given the form of a children's toy. Shaped like a gourd, his weight is where the Far Eastern mind/heart is: about two inches below the navel, in the "great sea of the belly." Being light-headed, therefore, this Daruma doll may be knocked in any way only to sway a while and then return upright. *Such is life,* says a popular poem of him: *Seven times down. Eight times up!* This Daruma does

not turn the other cheek; he is all cheek. Empty-headed, he is without fear, without tolerance or love for his fellow men. With only space inside, there is nothing to defend and so no one to attack. There is no virtue in this, no ideal of peace or nonviolence; he is upright by nature, but since he knows no "evil," he is in no way "good." He is what he is, and responds to whatever is: moving when it is needed, being still when it is not. Gravity is the root of his grace. The doll bears the stern face of the great Bodhidharma himself, but, as every child knows, it is only pretending; he plays at being a Sage only to seem a fool and so to bring smiles to one and all.

The real and revered Bodhidharma of Buddhist history, who came long ago from far away over the hills to China to stare for seven years at a wall, can seem a little ridiculous beside the toy that honors him, as Zen monks hell-bent upon Heaven can amuse plain folk. Liberation is said to be freedom from the illusion that one is bound; how then shall one discipline and bind oneself in order to be free? We have it on the authority of a Zen Master that "only men of will and might, brave enough to shoulder such a burden and to press straight forward without the slightest hesitation or timidity, will be able to enter it [the Tao]. For the rest of the people the chance is very very slight. An old proverb says: This matter is like one man against ten thousand enemies."[16]

A man of Zen, knowing himself as one of the rest of the people, must wonder at such parade-ground talk. How shall one enter by this straight and narrow path the way of Tao that is everywhere and nowhere? The original man of Tao, the old fellow Lao Tsu, confessed himself to be without will or might, as weak as water, and said of himself: "What a fool!"

BELOW. Sengai : *Bodhidharma* (Daruma). 18th c. Inscription reads: *Those honorable Buddhist scholars who love Buddha, leaving East, go westward (that is, to India); Mr. Daruma who dislikes Buddha, leaving West, comes eastward. I thought they might meet at the teahouse of awakening. But, woe is me! it was all a dream.*

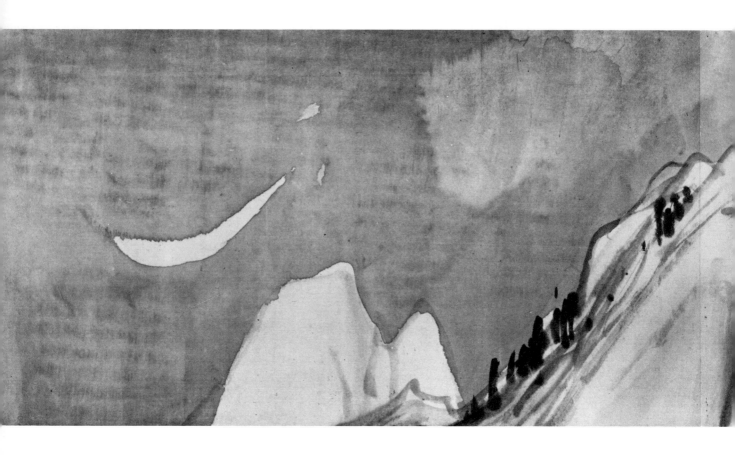

The man of Zen is such a fool. Without any desire for Enlightenment, without any high or solemn purpose, he wanders wherever the Way leads. It was in this way that a man of Zen was led one day to stand upon a hill. Three wise men at the foot of the hill saw him standing there. They wondered what he was doing and, each deciding differently, they began to argue among themselves. At last they climbed up to the man to find out who among them was right.

"Sir," said the first wise man, "we have wondered what it is that you are doing here, standing on this hill. Is it not perhaps because you have lost something? Your dog, perhaps?" The man of Zen shook his head.

"It is because you wish to enjoy the view," said the second wise man. "Surely it is to enjoy the beauties of nature that you are standing on this hill?" The man of Zen shook his head.

"Ah!" said the third wise man. "I know: it is not for any outward thing that you seek; it is an inward quest that occupies you. You are meditating on the Nature of things, are you not?" The man of Zen shook his head.

"What then?" asked the three wise men. "What are you doing here, standing on this hill?"

102

The man of Zen answered: "I am standing on this hill."

There are Wise Men of the East who say that all the many things of the world are unreal. Others will allow that they are relatively real: behind the many appearances is the one Reality. Science today can seem to confirm it, but that apparent Reality is unceasing *Change*. The one Reality appears as the many changing things—now for the while of an ever-resting mountain, now for the hour of a man, now for the minute of a mouse, for the instant of a midge. Reality *is* all these things and each of them, cosmos and cheese mite. Reality is not apart from the ten thousand things as the sun is not apart from its rays. To care for Reality, then, is to care for real things, each and every one, though frail as a spider's web, brief as a mayfly, insubstantial as morning mist. It takes a Wise Man to determine what is Real, what is unreal. Zen has no idea.

Suzuki Daisetz was asked by a student at a lecture once: "When you use the word *reality*, are you referring to the relative reality of the physical world, or to the Absolute Reality of the psychic world?" Saying nothing, Suzuki closed his eyes. ("Doing a Suzuki," the students called it, for at such times it could not be known whether he was profoundly meditating or just fast asleep.) After a full minute that seemed very much longer, Suzuki opened his eyes and said, "Yes!"[17]

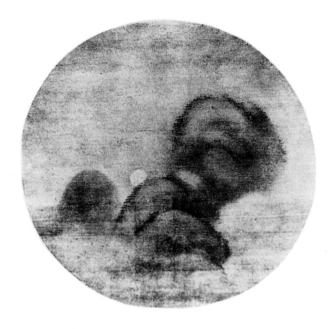

Yes! That is all that one can really say. Yes! to the living while we live. Yes! to all the ten thousand things about us. Yes! to death at the end. "Going to Paradise is good and to fall into Hell is also a matter for congratulation." One can try to say No, but this is at most to drag one's feet, and that resistance is all that unhappiness is, whatever its apparent cause or kind. In fact, we cannot say No to the world, for we *are* this world, and the unceasing change that is the nature of things changes us whether we will or no. We appear, and there's no stopping us until we cease to appear.

Things are what they *are,* and if they are illusory as some Wise Men of the East insist, well then, they *are* illusory. And so are we and any such statement we can make about things. Illusion then becomes our reality, and it becomes us to live as though life is real, even as a playing child lives abundantly in giving himself wholeheartedly to the illusion of being a real cop, a real robber, a cowboy, or an Indian really.

But children grow into philosophers and henceforth find it hard to play. It is understandable that some philosophers in our time should find life absurd. What is surprising, however, is that they should not find this cause for smiling. The absurdity of things is clear; if nothing else, zoos and parliaments prove it. And that men and women should be born at all, and

then live for a while only, only to die. . . . How absurd it all is! How wonderfully absurd! The solemnity of those philosophers who suffer and bemoan the absurdity of things can only mean that they see themselves separate and apart from it all, believing that all things are absurd *except* their saying so. It is similarly so with the religious who point to the passing of things as reason to turn from them. Buddhism sorrowfully points out that "all things are impermanent; all is subject to constant becoming." And why not?

How shall we avoid heat and cold? someone asked a man of Zen. He answered: "Be hot. Be cold." To be free of the pain of passing, it is necessary to be passing, to be what one actually and naturally is. Pain is pain—a simple painful fact. Suffering, however, is only and always the refusal of pain, the claim that life should *not* be painful; it is the rejection of a fact, the denial of life and of the nature of things. Death is the mind that minds dying. Where there is no fear of death, who is there to die?

There is no one, but there is still dying to be done, as the child well knows when it hears the bang! of the wooden gun. He dies then as he lived, and abundantly "bites the dust."

LEFT. Kao Jan-Hui : *Sunrise in the mountains.* 14th c. OPPOSITE. Seisetsu Seki : Last in the series of *Ten Cowherding Pictures.* 20th c. (See also copyright and title pages.)
Entering the City with Bliss-bestowing Hands. His humble cottage door is closed, and the wisest know him not. No glimpses of his inner life are to be caught; for he goes his own way without following the steps of the ancient sages. Carrying a gourd he goes out into the market; leaning on a stick he comes home. He is found in company with wine-bibbers and butchers; he and they are all converted into Buddhas.
Barechested and barefooted, he comes out into the marketplace;
Daubed with mud and ashes, how broadly he smiles!
There is no need for the miraculous power of the gods,
For he touches, and lo! the dead trees come into full bloom.

The meaning of life and death may be abstractly questioned, but it can be answered only in the way we live, the way we die. All men live and die, but here or there a man may at any moment awaken and do them *newly*, as for the first time. To live and to die is given to all creatures freely, as a matter of grace. The tiny wren, electric in the summer sun and then on frozen ground forever still, lives and dies in grace, naturally and inevitably. It is, however, given to man to live and die in awareness of this grace that is given to all creatures. Man is unique among creatures in his knowledge of death and in his laughter. Wonderfully then, he can even make of death a new thing: he can die with a smile.

When Teng Yin-feng was about to die, he said to those who mourned about him: "I have seen monks die sitting and lying, but has anyone died standing up?" Yes, some, he was told. "How about upside down?" he asked. No one had ever heard of such a thing! Teng Yin-feng stood on his head and died.

What is death then? What is life? What after all is Zen? What else can it be but life and death seen for what they *are:* Life itself. Life is the unexpected gift and unaccountable grace of all living and dying things. What is there then to strain after? Striving after Salvation, straining after Enlightenment is but greed and is always graceless, since it is the refusal of a gift.* What does a man of Zen have that another man does not? One thing only: *seeing.* All men have life but those who see that all men have life have it abundantly.

In spring, hundreds of flowers; in autumn, a
  harvest moon.
In summer, a refreshing breeze; in winter, snow.
If useless things do not hang in your mind,
any season is a good season. [18]

*Those who desire and strive for salvation most earnestly are in their zeal bound the more, since it is exactly their self-seeking that is giving them their pain. . . . When the Buddha extinguished ego in himself, the world burst into flower. But that, exactly, is the way it has always appeared to those in whom wonder—and not salvation—is religion. JOSEPH CAMPBELL : *Oriental Mythology.*

ABOVE. Shuko : *Sage riding a donkey.* 15th c.

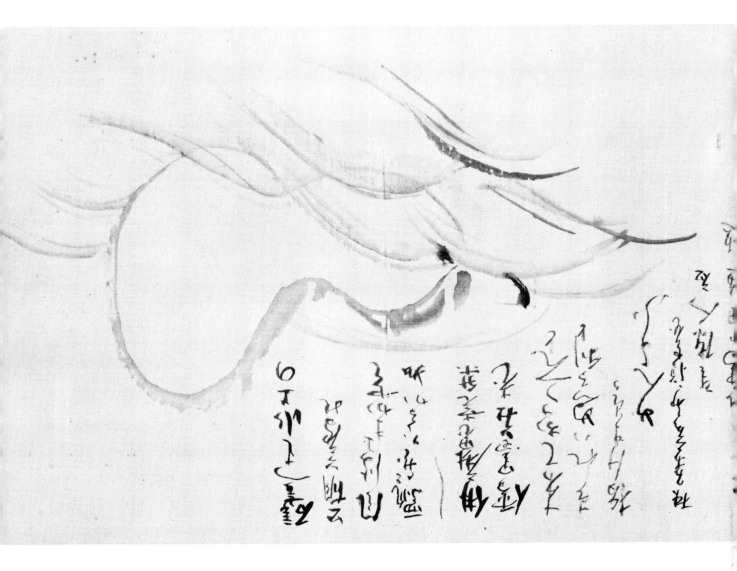

ABOVE. Sengai : *The floating gourd.* 18th c. Inscription reads: *It is like a gourd floating on the waters: it is never steady, now sinking, now rising, at the mercy of the winds. The gourd itself is altogether unconcerned. Buddha or Devil, Yao or Shun, Confucius or Mo-tzu, Lao-tzu or Chuang-tzu may all come to take hold of it. But the gourd will elusively slip out of their grasp. Amazing!*

Talk of Zen may seem useful for a while, but if it hangs in the mind we will fare no better in the four seasons. Talk of Zen may be useful if it proves how useless it is. What has been shown in these pages is that there is nothing of Zen in them. Words are for us things of use primarily, a means to meaning; but at their liveliest they are as life itself, meaningless; they are playthings, as balls from a juggler's hands, as spillings from a poet:

> You say that my poems are not poetry.
>   They are not.
> But if you see that they are not—
>   Why, there's the poetry! [19]

The same can be said of all that can be said of Zen. See that it is *not* Zen—Why, there's glory for you! Here's Zen!

But no. Even if it is the last word, Zen is still but a word. Away with it! What is left? What else but what *is?* "God—if I may borrow that word for a moment—the universe, and man are one indissoluble existence, one total whole," says Ruth Fuller Sasaki. "Only THIS—capital THIS—is. Anything and everything that appears to us as an individual entity or phenomenon, whether it be a planet or an atom, a mouse or a man, is but a temporary manifestation of THIS in form; every activity that takes place, whether it be birth or death, loving or eating breakfast, is but a temporary manifestation of THIS in activity."[20]

A manifestation is a manifestation, however temporary. A permanent manifestation would be as near to death as Life can get. There can be no more or less of THIS in a flash of lightning than in any Life Everlasting. THIS is all the while only and always *this* frog, *this* pond, *this* plop!, *this* man, *this* woman, *this* child, *this* sun and rain and rainbow, the birth of *this* owl, the death of *this* mouse, *this* rotting corpse by the roadside, *this* lively maggot emerging, *this* cuckoo calling now. . . .

The presence of things shows when "we" are present. "Men, though they must die, are not born in order to die, but in order to begin."[21] We begin *here,* with what is *now.* Unhappiness is the search for happiness, as the Devil is the want of God, and Hell is the need of Heaven. Where there is no seeking, there is no seeker; there is Nothing. . . . there is Space only, in which everything is, as it always is, waiting on us. Grace is given when we have the grace to receive it. The brightness of the day depends upon our awakening to it. *I am as one,* said Basho, *who eats his breakfast*

  gazing at the morning glories.

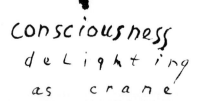

consciousness
  deLighting
    as crane

OPPOSITE AND LEFT. Paul Reps : Two *Zen Telegrams*.
20th c.

cucumber
unaccountably
cucumbering

REFERENCES

1. JAMES JEANS : *The Mysterious Universe*
2. CHUANG TSU : *Inner Chapters*
3. GROCK : *Grock: Life's a Lark*
4. A. S. EDDINGTON : *The Nature of the Physical World*
5. HOKOJI
6. LAURENCE BINYON : *The Spirit of Man in Asian Art*
7. IKKYU
8. Old poem, subject of a print by Harunobu, quoted in *The Flight of the Dragon* by LAURENCE BINYON
9. R. H. BLYTH : *Haiku*
10. CHRISTMAS HUMPHREYS : *Zen Buddhism*
11. FOSCO MARIANI : *Meeting with Japan*
12. D. T. ΑUZUKI : *Zen Buddhism and Its Influence on Japanese Culture*
13. R. H. BLYTH quoted in *The World of Zen* by NANCY WILSON ROSS
14. HERMANN KEYSERLING : *South American Meditations*
15. GAI EATON : *The Richest Vein*
16. MASTER HAN SHAN quoted in *The Practice of Zen* by GARMA C. C. CHANG
17. Reported by ALAN WATTS in *Does It Matter?*
18. WU-MEN
19. RYOKAN
20. RUTH FULLER SASAKI : *Zen: A Method for Religious Awakening*
21. HANNAH ARENDT : *The Human Condition*

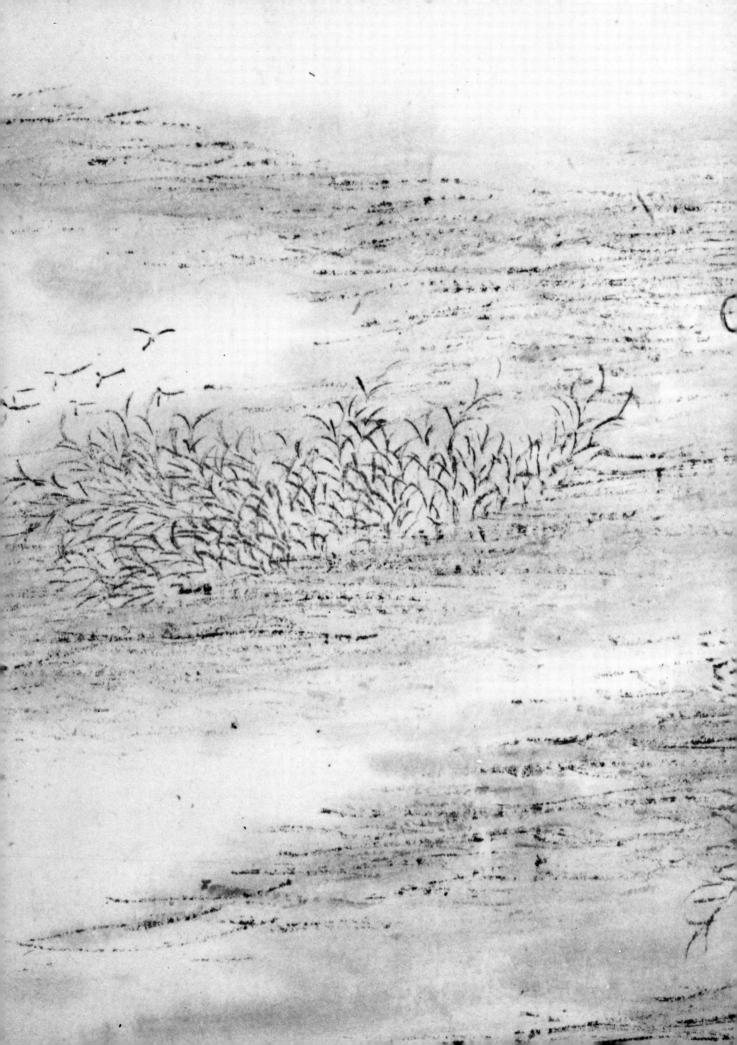

Michael Adam. Photograph by Leslie Silverlock

A NOTE ON THE TYPE
This book was set in Palatino, a type face designed by
Hermann Zapf in 1950. Bearing the name of a famous
penman of the sixteenth century, it ranks among the
Venetian romans, but is clearly an original and
contemporary type, not a mechanical copy of a historical
one.
Composed by UNIVERSITY GRAPHICS, INC.
Printed and bound by HALLIDAY LITHOGRAPHERS.
Typography and design by Kim Taylor.

PICTURE SOURCES & CREDITS

Sources for the illustrations in this book are given after their page numbers. Photographers' names appear in parentheses. Gratitude is expressed to all concerned.

FRONT COVER : *Zen Telegrams;* Charles E. Tuttle Company, Rutland, Vermont, and Tokyo, Japan
BACK COVER : Victoria and Albert Museum, London
ENDPAPERS : Neiraku Museum, Nara
TITLE PAGE : *Essays in Zen Buddhism;* Rider and Co., London, and Grove Press, New York
DEDICATION & CONTENTS PAGES : *The Tao of Painting;* Pantheon Books, New York
1 : Victoria and Albert Museum, London
3 : The Ark Press, Penzance, Cornwall
6 : The Ark Press, Penzance, Cornwall
9 : Victoria and Albert Museum, London
10 : *The Art of Indian Asia;* Pantheon Books, New York. (Eliot Elisofon) Courtesy Edward I. Elicofon
12 : Victoria and Albert Museum, London
13 : *Kama Kala;* Nagel Publishers, Geneva. (D. H. Sahiar)
16 : (Sunil Janah)
17, 18L, 18R, 19 : Victoria and Albert Museum, London
20 : Collection of Raja Druv Chand of Lambagraon, Kangra Valley. *Basholi Painting;* Publications Division, Ministry of Information and Broadcasting, Government of India, Delhi
21L : Collection of Ajit Mookerjee
21R, 22 top : Victoria and Albert Museum, London
22 bottom : Collection of Municipal Museum, Allahabad. *Kangra Paintings of Love;* National Museum, New Delhi
23 : *Kama Kala;* Nagel Publishers, Geneva
24L, 24R : Victoria and Albert Museum, London
25L, 25R : David Kung
26 : Birmingham Museum and Art Gallery, Birmingham, England
27 : Victoria and Albert Museum, London
28L, 28R : Collection of Ajit Mookerjee
29 : Victoria and Albert Museum, London
30 : Nelson Gallery–Atkins Museum, Kansas City, Missouri
32 : Victoria and Albert Museum, London
33 top : Collection of Provincial Museum, Lucknow. *Basholi Painting;* Publications Division, Ministry of Information and Broadcasting, Government of India, Delhi
33 bottom, 34 : Victoria and Albert Museum, London
35, 36 : Collection of Kishangarh Darbar. *Kishangarh Painting;* Lalit Kala Akademi, New Delhi
39 : *The Tao of Painting;* Pantheon Books, New York
40 : The Cleveland Museum of Art, John L. Severance Fund, Ohio
43 : British Museum, London
44 : Collection of Chuang-tao-ko. *Meisterwerke Chinesischer Tuschezeichnungen;* Verlag Amstutz, Herdeg & Co., Zurich
46 : British Museum, London
47 : Collection of Charles A. Drenowatz, Zurich. *Fantastics and Eccentrics in Chinese Painting;* Asia Society Inc., New York
48 : Tokyo National Museum, Tokyo
50, 51 : Hale Observatories, Pasadena, California
52–53 : The Smithsonian Institution, Freer Gallery of Art, Washington, D.C.
54, 55 : The Sumitomo Collection, Kyoto
56 : Collection of Chuang-tao-ko. *Meisterwerke Chinesischer Tuschezeichnungen;* Verlag Amstutz, Herdeg & Co., Zurich
57 : Nelson Gallery–Atkins Museum, Kansas City, Missouri
58 : British Museum, London
59 : National Palace Museum, Taichung, Taiwan
61 : Ross Collection, Courtesy Museum of Fine Arts, Boston
62 : British Museum, London
65 : Tokyo National Museum, Tokyo
66 : Nelson Gallery–Atkins Museum, Kansas City, Missouri
67, 69 : British Museum, London
70 : National Palace Museum, Taichung, Taiwan
71 : Collection of Chuang-tao-ko. *Meisterwerke Chinesischer Tuschezeichnungen;* Verlag Amstutz, Herdeg & Co., Zurich
73 : Ross Collection. Courtesy Museum of Fine Arts, Boston
74–75 : British Museum, London
76 : Kosetsu Museum of Art, Kobe
79 : *Zen Flesh, Zen Bones;* Charles E. Tuttle Co., Rutland, Vermont, and Tokyo, Japan
80, 82–83 : The Smithsonian Institution, Freer Gallery of Art, Washington, D.C.
84 : Idemitsu Art Gallery, Tokyo. Matsugaoka Bunke Foundation, Tokyo
85 : National Museum of Korea, Seoul
86 : The Cleveland Museum of Art, Norman O. Stone and Ella A. Stone Memorial Fund, Ohio
87 : Private collection, Japan. *Meisterwerke Chinesischer Malerei;* Safari-Verlag, Berlin
88L : *Zen and Zen Classics.* The Hokuseido Press, Japan
88R : National Palace Museum, Taichung, Taiwan
89, 90L, 90R, 91 : British Museum, London
92L : Japanese Information Centre, London
94 : Japanese National Tourist Organisation, London
95 : Japanese Information Centre, London
96L : Eisei Bunko Foundation, Hosokawa Collection, Tokyo
96R : *Zen from the West* by Sohaku Ogata, Rider and Co., London
97 : Tokyo National Museum, Tokyo
98 : Idemetsu Art Gallery, Tokyo. Matsugaoka Bunke Foundation, Tokyo
99 : British Museum, London
100L : Collection of Sainen-ji Temple, Japan
100R : Japanese National Tourist Office, London
101 : Idemetsu Art Gallery, Tokyo. Matsugaoka Bunke Foundation, Tokyo
102–103 : Private collection, Japan
104 : Collection of Konji-in Temple, Kyoto
105 : *Essays in Zen Buddhism.* Rider and Co., London, and Grove Press, New York
106 : Bigelow Collection. Courtesy Museum of Fine Arts, Boston
107 : Idemetsu Art Gallery, Tokyo, Matsugaoka Bunke Foundation, Tokyo
108, 109 : *Zen Telegrams.* Charles E. Tuttle Co., Rutland, Vermont, and Tokyo, Japan

ACKNOWLEDGMENTS

Gratitude is expressed to the following publishers for the use of textual material as listed.
Copyright page and page 104 : Translation from verse and commentary to the *Ten Cow-Herding Pictures* from *Essays in Zen Buddhism* by D. T. Suzuki. Rider and Co., London, and Grove Press, New York
Pages 33 and 49 : Lines from *Duino Elegies* by Rainer Maria Rilke, translated by J. B. Leishman and Stephen Spender. St. John's College, Oxford; Hogarth Press, London, and New Directions, New York
Pages 84, 96, 99, 101, 107 : Translations and comments by D. T. Suzuki from *Sengai, The Zen Master;* The Matsugaoka Bunke Foundation, Tokyo, and Faber and Faber, London